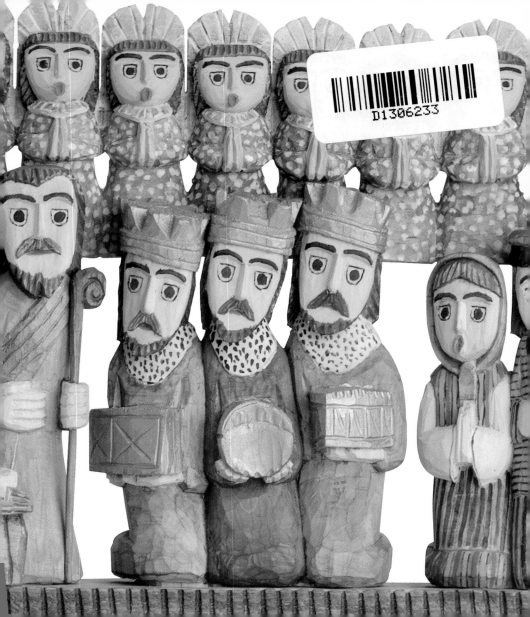

ART
OF
THE
CRÈCHE

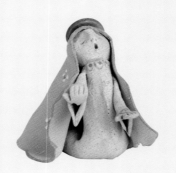

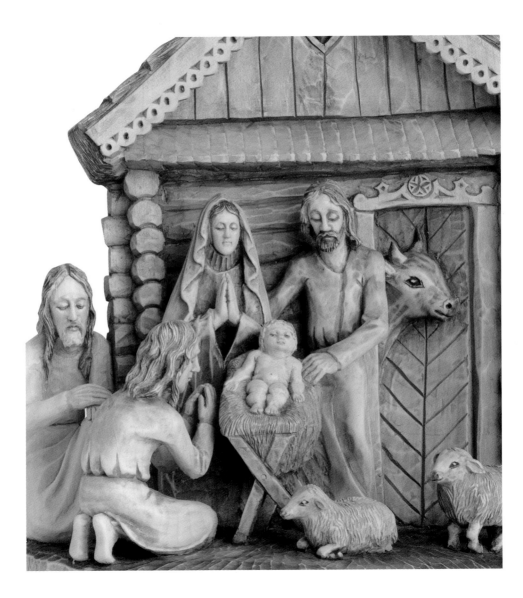

ART
OF
THE
CRÈCHE

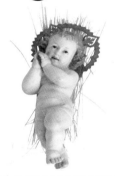

NATIVITIES
FROM
AROUND
THE
WORLD

JAMES L. GOVAN

MERRELL

LONDON · NEW YORK

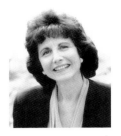

EMILIA LONGOBARDO GOVAN (1937–2000)

I dedicate this book to Emilia, my loving wife and friend of thirty-eight years and the caring mother of our two sons, Michael and Stephen. Emilia was an avid partner in building our family's collection of crèches. A radiant individual, she reflected an openness to life and people that made her an instant friend to many who met her. She was an extremely talented person who, during an accomplished career, was a college teacher, a citizen leader, a manager in the legislative and executive branches of the U.S. Government, a lawyer, and a consultant. For her citizen leadership in transportation and environmental issues, she was recognized as a Washingtonian of the Year in 1974, and for her professional achievements in the fields of energy and environment, she was awarded an honorary Doctor of Laws degree by her alma mater, St. Joseph's College of New York, in 1992. She would have been pleased to know that our collection of crèches was to be shared with so many.

OPPOSITE: Emilia received this Bambino from her mother, Anna Longobardo, who brought it to the United States from Italy in 1937.

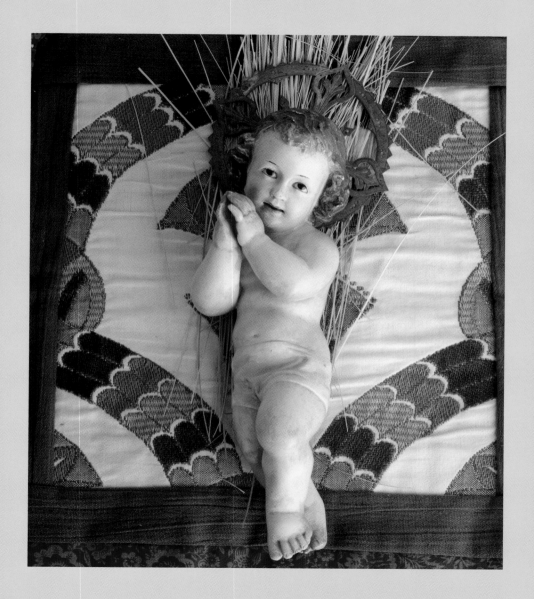

CONTENTS

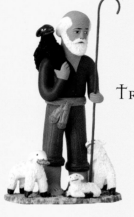

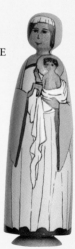

A COLLECTOR'S JOURNEY
COLLECTING STORIES

Christmas abounds with traditions, one of the most enduring of which is the nativity scene, or "crèche" (a French term meaning "crib"), the portrayal of the Nativity through figurines of people and animals. My late wife, Emilia, and I began collecting crèches in the 1970s. As the collection grew, so did our interest in the tradition's development and scope, and the experience of collecting became a journey. Our search for nativities reached all corners of the world, through both travel and the marvel of modern communications. We engaged museum curators, merchants, missionaries, friends (many of them working abroad), and artists. The richness of the social context was an unexpected joy. We encountered many interesting people, if only briefly, and gained insights into many cultures.

The collection consists of more than 450 crèches from over a hundred countries, and reflects the relatively recent spread of the tradition (only three were made before 1960).

Some older examples are so prized that only museums and a few fortunate private collectors possess them. While the collection bears the family name, it is really the product of many people. In one year, for example, we received crèches from each of four former colleagues working in Africa; a Catholic priest in Arizona; a New Zealand carver I knew only through e-mail; and some dear family friends working in Hungary. Emilia and I saw ourselves as simply the caretakers of a wonderful collection created by many others.

I intend to present the crèches with two parallel themes. The first represents, for me, how the Nativity story has been accepted by cultures the world over. People see themselves as part of the story: the figures appear in local dress among scenes with familiar animals and plants, and gifts for Jesus are those important or common to that culture. The second theme demonstrates how crèches create bonds within and among different cultures, whether by the giving of crèches or

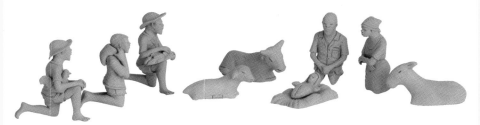

by the devotion of several generations of a family to their creation. Many pieces are gifts: some from people I know, some from those I've never met. As the tradition spreads around the world, people—Christian and non-Christian, rich and poor—are linked by artisans earning a living. The art of the crèche symbolizes the world's cultural diversity and richness just as it symbolizes a common humanity among all peoples.

THE REWARDING ART OF COLLECTING

Collecting is far more than acquiring objects. It embraces not only the search for the objects, but also research into their individual backgrounds, appreciation of their attributes, and understanding of their social contexts. I was encouraged by the richness of our experience, and by the reactions of many who have seen portions of the collection exhibited, to include here some description of the way in which it grew.

Emilia and I did not plan to build a collection of crèches. We were drawn to the idea after acquiring three over several years. The first was a traditional Italian scene acquired for Christmas shortly after our marriage in 1962. The second, bought a few years later, was a whimsical Portuguese scene.

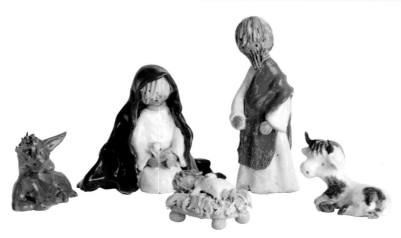

The third, obtained in 1974, was a slightly abstract American crèche. While looking at the figurines from this American set in a shop, we discussed how imaginatively and differently people of various cultures have created the appealing scene. One of us—I do not recall which—asked what we would do with three crèches. The other replied, "Well, we might collect them." So we decided, twelve years after acquiring the Italian set, to begin our collection.

Three main influences prompted us. First was a shared Catholic faith that gave the Nativity of Christ special meaning for us. Second was our strong and eclectic interest in art (for me, especially folk art). Third was a fascination with cultural diversity. Both Emilia and I had immigrant backgrounds: she grew up in an Italian section of Brooklyn, with parents who came from Procida, a small island in the Bay of Naples; and I grew up in a neighborhood of Eastern European immigrants that included my Lithuanian grandparents. I was eventually drawn to a career in international affairs.

FROM COLLECTION TO EXHIBITION

The character of the collection developed slowly at first. By the early 1980s, there were only twenty-five crèches: the demands of work and family allowed us little time for collecting, and we had limited means or time for travel. While initially we wanted to seek out nativities from diverse cultures to reflect the universality of the tradition, a critical focus was also to acquire pieces that were fine examples of art. We passed up many crèches in shops each Christmas in our determination to be selective.

During the 1980s, we became interested in learning about the historical development of the crèche tradition, and gathered materials on folk art and related cultural traditions. By the late 1980s, the collection had grown to roughly one hundred pieces. I became more committed to documenting them, learning as much as possible about how they were made and the individuals who made them. In some cases, I was lucky enough to talk to the makers themselves. By then, we had more opportunities to travel abroad, and we continued our search wherever we went.

By 1990, the collection had grown too large to be exhibited in our home. We began to explore the possibility of exhibiting elsewhere to stimulate interest in the tradition. Disappointed by the limited information available in English, we also began to consider writing a book about the tradition and our collection. Given the growth of the collection, the desire to find special crèches—especially fine works of art— became stronger, and we decided to look for opportunities to commission works. We focused on locating gifted artists and crèches of certain cultures, and continued to travel, both abroad and in the United States. As a result, by 2000,

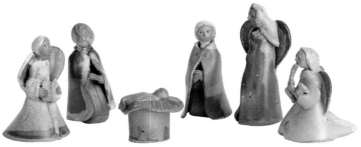

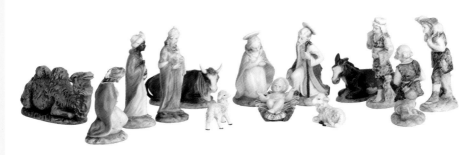

the collection exceeded 260 crèches and had been exhibited publicly several times; nearly thirty crèches had been commissioned; and a book was under way.

The first opportunity to exhibit came in 1990, at the Paul VI Institute for the Arts in Washington, D.C., by invitation of its director, Monsignor Michael di Teccia Farina. We had first contacted Monsignor Farina in 1986 and acquired two wonderful crèches from him: one by a Belgian nun, Sister Angelica; the other—one of our finest and most admired—by a Parisian artist, Noëlle Fabri-Canti (see pages 238–39). This acquaintance led not only to other exhibitions, but also to a rewarding friendship. Monsignor Farina's support and that of the Pope John Paul II Cultural Center, which provided an exhibition venue for five years (2001–2005), have been instrumental in helping the collection gain public recognition.

The process of building the collection has involved scores of people worldwide, and so I think of it as belonging to many who were part of its development. When I look at the crèches, I see first of all the artists' interpretations of the wondrous event of Christ's birth. But many also represent touching personal experiences. The crèche's religious, artistic, and cultural dimensions exist in a social context.

This context includes encounters with artists. For instance, the generosity of Lilia Shevchenko, a poor woman in Vladivostok, Russia, who made her first nativity and then gave it to me—even though we had never met—humbled me. The same is true of Geoff Pryor in New Zealand, who was so pleased to create a nativity in the Maori tradition that he presented it to me as a gift. There is Nicario Jiménez Quispe of Peru, from whom we commissioned one large nativity, but who made two. I was enriched by engaging with yet other artists: a third-generation firefighter from Texas, Alfredo Rodriguez, who devotes himself to preserving the Spanish Colonial tradition of carving *santos*—saints or religious figures; Hanneke Ippisch, who served in the Dutch resistance; and the retired professor

Mitsuki Kumekawa in Japan, who accepted my request to make a nativity and expressed the honor he felt in doing so, despite not being a Christian.

The stories of people who made special efforts to contribute give deeper meaning to many crèches. A museum curator in Croatia, Josip Barlek, had a nativity scene made for me by an artist who is one of only a few still working in a particular regional style. In Young Cho, a Jesuit Brother in Cambodia, engaged several carvers (some of them land-mine victims) who strove meticulously for eight months to make a nativity with Khmer features. Our one-time tour guide in the Czech Republic, Václav Lojka— interpreter, shipping agent, and friend—helped acquire several crèches there. Many friends presented us with nativities acquired on their travels.

The generosity of many former colleagues at the U.S. Agency for International Development (USAID) touched me deeply. Working all over the world, but primarily in Africa, they sought out artisans and commissioned crèches, often presenting them to me as gifts. Others bought them for me on their travels to other countries. And my office staff commissioned a Kenyan nativity for me as a retirement gift.

jOYFUL EXPERiENCE

Emilia and I could never have foreseen how the collection would affect our lives. My Christian faith deepened as I enjoyed encounters with Muslim, Taoist, Buddhist, Jew, and those of no affiliation, who created nativities. Beyond devoting my career to USAID, I learned more about world cultures while forming the collection. I connected with my ancestral roots in Lithuania. And in the forming of Friends of the Creche, a national society devoted to the nativity tradition, I gained friends from across the country, increased my knowledge, and shared the enjoyment of the tradition.

Above all, the building of the collection brought great joy to Emilia and me. In her last months, she made me promise to carry on with it. So I do. It represents a special facet of a lifetime shared in so many ways, and to me is imbued with the beauty of the care that Emilia bestowed upon it and the delight it gave her.

SIGN & SYMBOL

✦

NATIVITY, INCARNATION, AND EUCHARIST

The accounts of Christ's birth in the Gospels of Luke and Matthew are familiar to every Christian, and provide the basic iconography of the event. Christ is born in Bethlehem and lies in a manger, possibly in a stable, but certainly where animals might be present or near by. An angel announces the good news to shepherds guarding their flock. They rush to see the Infant. They are the first to witness the event, and they leave, glorifying God. In time, magi from the East follow a star that leads them to the newborn king. On finding him, they offer gifts and pay homage.

Each reader of the Nativity story forms an image of this event, an image probably influenced by representations in art—paintings, sculptures, icons, and myriad other art

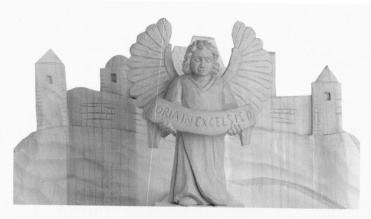

forms. This volume illustrates a few of the many variations of the scene that artists have used to depict the story. Whatever the image, however, Christians see the Nativity as the mystery of the Incarnation, the union of the divine and human in Jesus Christ. It is an expression of faith that has been reflected in art through the centuries.

Belief in the Incarnation has shaped articles of faith and religious rituals and devotions, so it is not surprising that some crèches explicitly allude to or include signs and symbols of Christianity. In the Venezuelan nativity (see pages 24–25), for example, the artist uses a chalice for the Infant's manger, evoking the moment of consecration in the Catholic Mass.

CZECH REPUBLIC

✦

JAROSLAV FRENCL

BETHLEHEM

In 1999—searching for a Czech crèche—Emilia and I visited České Budějovice, where, at a market, Jaroslav Frencl was displaying his carvings: all crèches. Our guide, Václav Lojka, offered to help us acquire one, and through him, Frencl sent us pictures of his work. Václav collected our chosen crèche from Frencl's studio and arranged delivery. Born in 1960 in Horni Dvoriste, Frencl taught himself to carve at the age of ten, using books and inspired by Gothic and Baroque crèches. "Everything depends on the wood," he says; he instinctively "knows" what kind of scene he will carve from each piece. His scenes are made using hand tools. He established a studio shortly after the collapse of Communism in his country, and, as well as crèches, carves works for churches and public spaces. His crèches often feature architectural settings, such as Bethlehem in this scene, which presents the basic iconography of the Nativity.

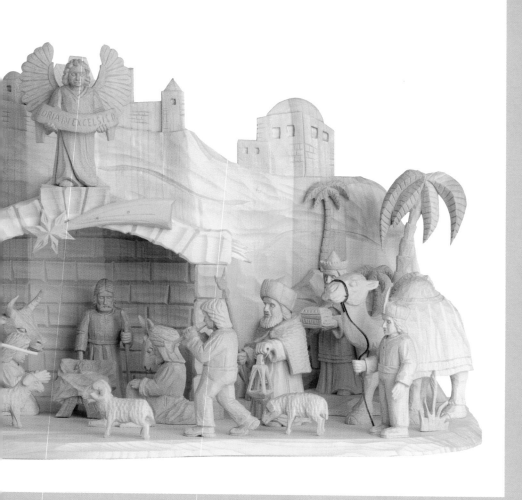

MASSACHUSETTS, USA
+
MARY FULLER

HOUSE OF BREAD

Mary Fuller was inspired to make this scene by a nativity she was given by her daughter-in-law. It was a "bread nativity," found at a craft fair around 1990. Fuller adapted the design and has since made many pieces like it, usually as gifts. She took the piece's title from "Bethlehem," which is composed of two Hebrew words, *Bet* ("house") and *Lechem* ("bread").

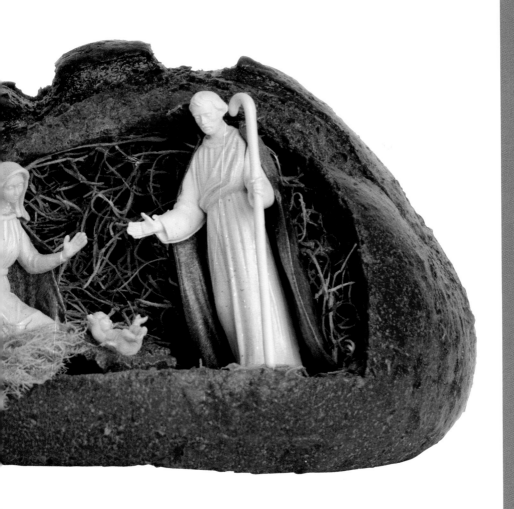

VENEZUELA

+

MLuisaR

CHRIST IN CHALICE

This triptych comes from the Venezuelan state of Mérida. The style resembles that of work from a wood-carving center in Tabay, but nothing is known about the carver who marked the piece "MLuisaR." When closed, the crèche reveals it has been carved from a single tree trunk or branch. The composition is one of the most unusual depictions of the Christ Child in the collection. His manger, a chalice, suggests the sacred moment of consecration in the Mass: the changing of bread and wine into the body and blood of Christ. One angel, the largest, portrayed in half-body form, seems to float on a cloud. Among several smaller ones, appearing with only childlike heads and wings, are a black and a white angel joined together above the Infant, possibly symbolizing harmony among people.

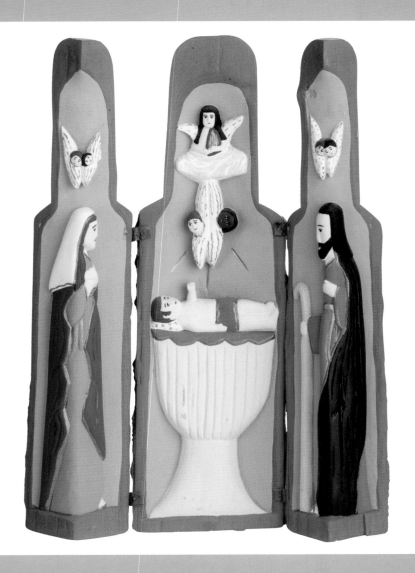

PORTUGAL/CALIFORNIA, USA
QUIRINA/ROBERT DAVIS
THE ALTAR

This rendition emphasizes the Eucharist's symbolism by presenting the figures on an altar. The form, which originated in the late 1920s in Estremoz (east of Lisbon), is now traditional locally. It was inspired by the presentation of popular saints at festivals on staircase thrones.

The clay figures are arranged traditionally: kings at the top, Holy Family in the middle, shepherds below. The shepherds wear nineteenth-century Estremoz regional clothes, and chickens perch on the manger, underlining the humble setting.

The figures and altar were acquired separately. In the early 1990s, one of Emilia's colleagues brought back from Portugal figures signed "Quirina," an important artisan in Estremoz. I discovered that the figures often sit on an altar, and, some years later, I asked friends traveling to Portugal to bring back an altar piece. The altars Robert and Judith Davis saw were too heavy and fragile for shipping, so Robert himself made this altar for me as a gift.

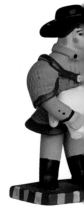

26

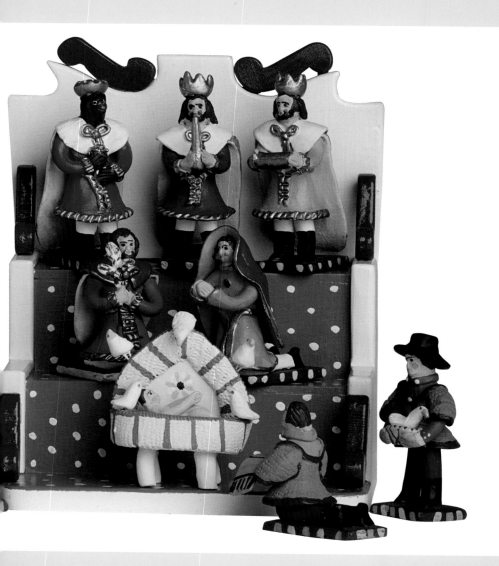

TEXAS, USA
✦
ALFREDO RODRÍGUEZ
THE POWERFUL HAND

I commissioned Alfredo Rodriguez's first crèche in 1995 (see pages 48–49). We stayed in touch, and Alfredo later introduced me to the Hispanic image *La Mano Poderosa*, "The Powerful Hand." This image, the hand of God, depicts Christ's stigmata and a traditional grouping of the Holy Family and Mary's parents. Sometimes saints' images are included at the base of the hand.

In 2005, I asked Alfredo to carve such an image in memory of Emilia, with an emphasis on the Nativity, by presenting Christ as an infant instead of as a young child (as is more common). I wished to include St. Francis, as a link to the crèche tradition, and St. Anthony of Padua, to whom Emilia held a special devotion. Mary is to the Infant's right, and St. Ann (her mother) is on the little finger; to Jesus's left is St. Joseph with a flowering staff, and on the thumb is St. Joachim (Mary's father). St. Francis holds a cross; a bird perches on his other hand. Jesus stands on a Bible in St. Anthony's left hand.

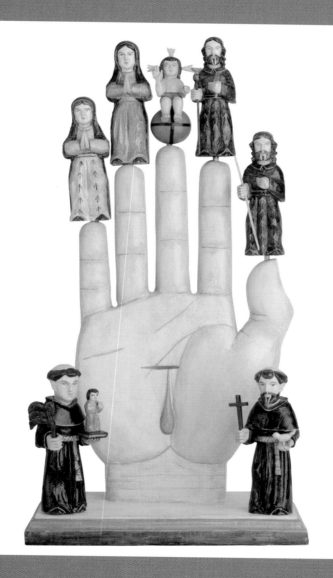

WHAT CHILD IS THIS?

✦

THE EVOLUTION OF ARTISTIC EXPRESSION

St. Francis of Assisi is often credited with creating the first crèche scene—on Christmas Eve, 1223. Other notable depictions show that representations of the Nativity have long been part of Christian tradition. Scenes of the Adoration of the Magi, perhaps dating from the late second century, were found in Roman catacombs. From around 1290, nativity sculptures by Arnolfo di Cambio graced the first church dedicated to Mary, Mother of God—Santa Maria Maggiore in Rome—and parts of this sculptural grouping can still be found there today. Di Cambio's work has traditionally been considered the earliest known three-dimensional crèche, although recent scholarship suggests that a crèche in a church in Bologna and another in Venice may date to around 1250 or earlier.

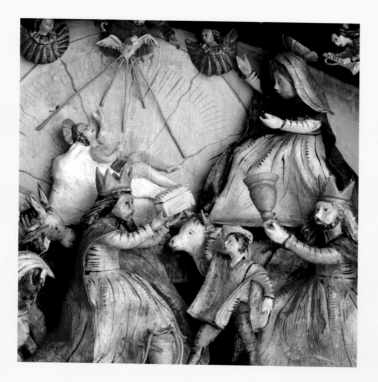

Though it began in Italy, the tradition of three-dimensional depictions of the Nativity eventually spread through Europe. When this tradition was, in turn, brought to other parts of the world, it was further embellished and enhanced by local imagination and artistic tastes.

ITALY
✦
CLAUDIO RISO

PRESEPIO

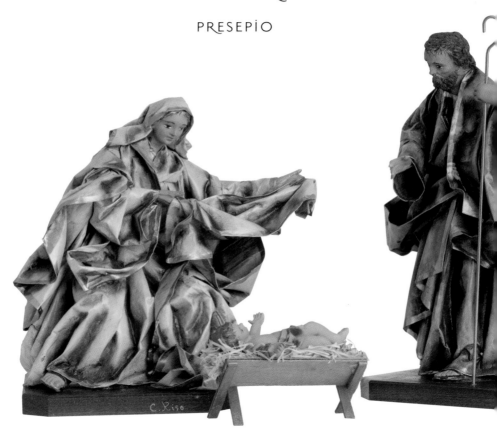

Emilia and I found this *cartapesta* (papier-mâché) crèche or *presepio* in Claudio Riso's family studio in Lecce in 1995, and Riso demonstrated the technique to us. Straw figures are coated in layers of glue-soaked paper, which is worked while wet, then smoothed with a hot iron. A thin layer of plaster is applied, and the figure finished with oil paints. This beautiful crèche illustrates the versatility of the process. Flowing lines define the forms of Mary and Joseph: Mary places a blanket on the Christ Child and Joseph turns toward him. The Infant's extended arms create a classic pose, symbolic of his reaching out to humanity. Mary and Joseph's clothing is colored, but Lecce artisans generally favor the less colorful, brownish garb of the Infant.

Claudio Riso (born in Bari in 1966) developed an interest in the art of *cartapesta* at an early age. He worked in the studio of Antonio Malecore, one of the leading *cartapesta* artists of the twentieth century, in Lecce. Riso has been creating crèche figures for more than two decades.

PERU

NICARIO JIMÉNEZ QUISPE

RETABLO

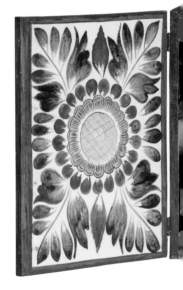

The *retablo* art form (literally "behind the altar") was brought to the New World by Spanish missionaries. *Retablos* are images of holy figures painted on flat panels, or are box-like forms containing devotional figures, for use as a portable altar or shrine. In the Andean region, the portable *retablo* custom waned in the early twentieth century, but was revived mid-century by Joaquín López Antay, who transformed the *retablo* from a devotional icon into an expression of both secular and religious subjects. In reviving an art form steeped in tradition, López Antay and others, including Nicario Jiménez Quispe (born 1957), who made this crèche, gained respect as leading Andean folk artists (see also pages 154–55).

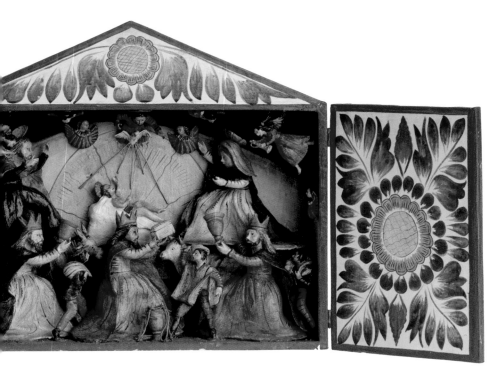

Jiménez's nativity depicts a traditional composition of the Adoration of the Magi, with shepherds in Andean dress, and angels filling the sky. God, the Father, and a dove representing the Holy Spirit look down on the Christ Child.

POLAND
✦
JACEK GŁUCH

KRAKOVIAN SZOPKA

The convent of St. Clare in Krakow owns fourteenth-century nativity figures possibly brought by Franciscan friars. Early crèches consisted of the traditional figures; puppets introduced in the Baroque period were soon set in three-dimensional structures that provided scenes for nativity plays, and in nineteenth-century Krakow, these became known as the Krakovian crib, or *szopka*. In the twentieth century, stationary figures replaced the puppets. Today the *szopki* are set in splendid structures that reflect Krakow's buildings, and are celebrated each December in a competition dating from 1937. In the 1960s, the late Witold Głuch became a prize-winning *szopka* artist; his son, Jacek, is also a competition winner. Here Jacek uses traditional *szopki* materials—cardboard and paper—with tinfoil and light wood, and wooden religious figures. Typically, the Holy Family is at the top; here the lower level is left empty, although it often contains figures, both religious and secular.

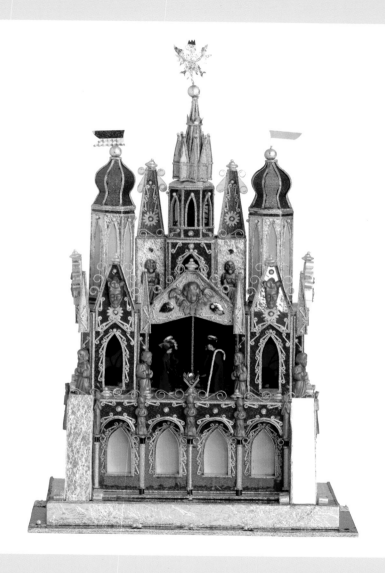

GERMANY

UNKNOWN ARTIST

PYRAMID

A unique style of crèche, often called "pyramid" because of its shape, appeared in the Erzgebirge region of eastern Germany in the eighteenth century. These crèches have one or more tiers of nativity figures, and are topped with a fanlike piece that, when powered by the heat from lighted candles on the lowest level, turns the other tiers to produce a parade of figures. The pyramidal form reflects the region's mountains, which were mined for silver, tin, and other ores. Some miners took up carving in their off season; eventually, as mines closed, carving became the principal source of income. Artisans are still making crèches in such towns as Seiffen and Schneeberg.

In this scene, kings surround the Holy Family on the first tier, shepherds occupy the second, and angels blow their horns in celebration on the top tier. Another family owned this nativity for about thirty years before it was given to me for the collection.

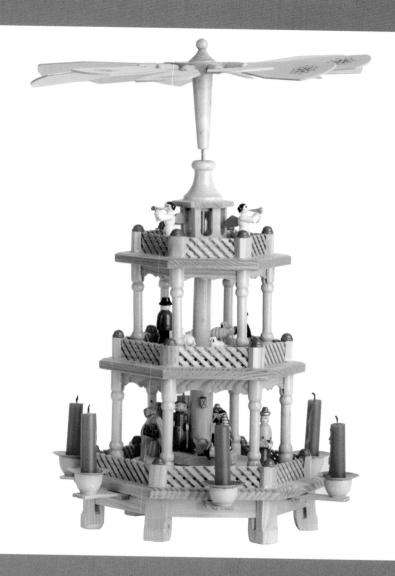

MEXICO
UNKNOWN ARTIST
ARBOL DE LA VIDA

In Metepec, not far from Mexico City, artists follow a tradition of creating clay models of a fanciful scene known as *Arbol de la Vida*, the "Tree of Life." The inspiration for this art form, which has been associated with fertility and life, is unclear. Some suggest that the origin of the Tree of Life dates back to pre-Hispanic influences; some suggest it was inspired by Franciscan teachings; yet others assert that this particular imagery was a twentieth-century development. These treelike forms, with branches, vines, and sometimes flowers, contain religious and secular scenes. Initially the religious images often depicted Adam and Eve, but other biblical scenes, including the Nativity, became common. The models were often made in the form of candelabra and incense burners to be used in weddings and other ceremonies.

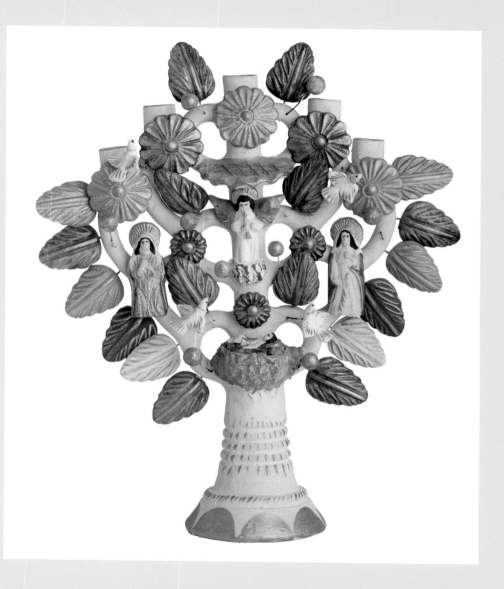

MEXICO
✦
JUAN HERNÁNDEZ ARZALUZ

ARBOL DE LA VIDA

Juan Hernández Arzaluz of Metepec is gaining recognition for his intriguing Trees of Life. In 1997, he was awarded one of Mexico's most prestigious artistic awards, the Galardón Nacional de Tlaquepaque, Jalisco. Hernández is known for portraying such scenes as the Nativity and Noah's Ark, as well as everyday Mexican life. He began modeling with clay at seven, and started making Trees of Life at fifteen. Now in his thirties, he says "Nativity Trees are one of my favorite pieces to make."

Hernández's incredibly detailed miniature trees are typically just 8 or 9 inches (20 or 23 cm) tall, but this one, which I commissioned, is 12 inches (30 cm) high. It is fashioned in the traditional form of a candelabrum. The Holy Family and angel greet the kings, who arrive on an elephant, a horse, and a camel—a depiction common to Mexican portrayals of the magi. The sun, the moon, butterflies, birds, and sunflowers adorn the Tree of Life.

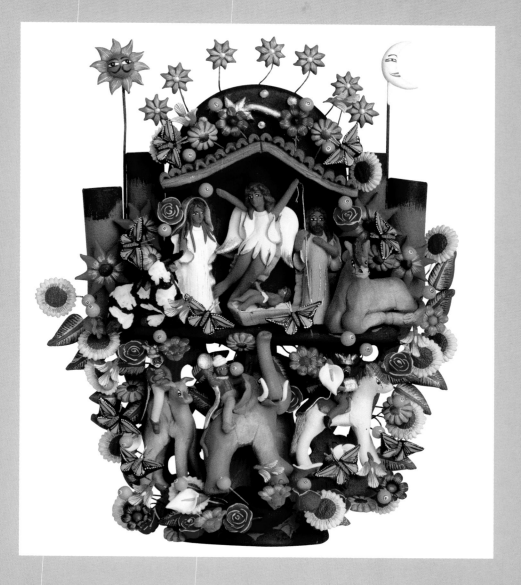

Tanzania
Unknown Artist
Makonde Carving

Wood carving has always been important to the Makonde people, who live in the coastal border region of Tanzania and Mozambique, since their tribal belief is that the first Makonde woman came to life from a carving. Contemporary pieces are abstract, but still reflect beliefs and customs. Since the arrival of Christian missionaries in the 1920s, Makonde carvers have created many items for churches, gaining acclaim for their carvings of Christian themes, especially crèches.

This example is by an artisan associated with a Benedictine mission in Mtwara, Tanzania; I acquired it in Nairobi, Kenya, in 1985. It is one of the most delicately carved crèches in the collection, and it is sad not to know who made it. Like most Makonde carvings, it is made from

44

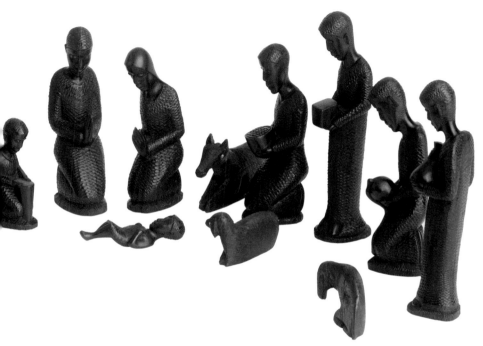

the heartwood of the African blackwood, or *mpingo*, tree, a heavy, dense, finely grained wood. The artist combines indigenous animals and musical instruments with traditional crèche elements, such as the shepherd carrying a sheep across his shoulder. The exquisitely carved, silky-smooth figures convey a sense of deep adoration.

FRANCE

SANTONS MARCEL CARBONEL

SANTONS

Clay *santons* ("little saints") represent the rural people of Provence, and those who make them are called *santonniers*. The custom began as a reaction to the French Revolution, which had suppressed religion, and the figures became more readily available after 1798, when molds were first used. *Santons* are made either of clay (in which case, they are usually less than 6 inches/15 cm tall) or of

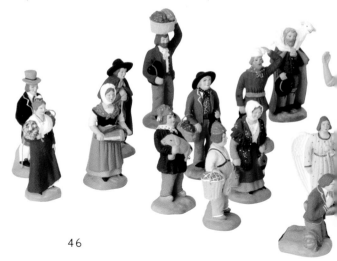

cloth. Cloth figures may be 12 inches (30 cm) or taller. The tradition was reinvigorated in the twentieth century, particularly through the work of the late Marcel Carbonel and his family after 1935. Carbonel was the first to fire the clay figures, making them more durable than earlier dried-clay examples.

The Holy Family and magi, presented traditionally here, are accompanied by exquisitely hand-painted Provençal villagers in period costume, offering the fruits of their labors. With fewer than forty figures and no buildings, this scene does not fully convey the range or setting of Carbonel's village of worshippers, but it illustrates the diversity of the gathering and the skilled work on each piece.

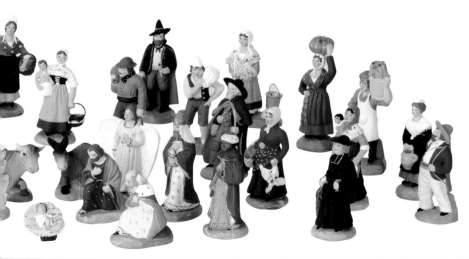

TEXAS, USA
✦
ALFREDO RODRIGUEZ
SANTOS

In the southwestern United States, Latin America, and the Philippines, a Spanish tradition exists of carving *santos* ("saints"). Unlike French *santons*, which developed into secular figures, *santos* remain exclusively depictions of saints. In this tradition is the crèche—his first—I commissioned from Alfredo Rodriguez (see also pages 28–29), a retired firefighter and self-taught carver in San Antonio. The revival of local Spanish Colonial carving practices is important to him, and he works to promote the *santos* tradition. He uses Colonial methods, traditional wood, and homemade tools like those of the Colonial period. Natural gesso, water-based pigment, and pine shellac finish the simple, characterful figures with strong colors. The inclusion of a rooster in this scene reflects a

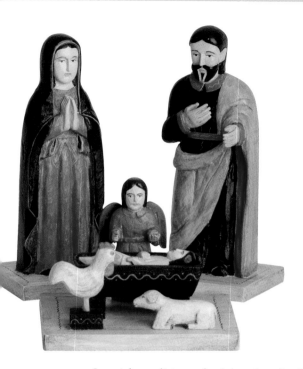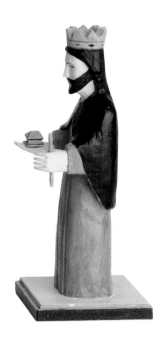

Spanish tradition of celebrating the first Mass of Christmas as the Mass of the Rooster; it is said that the only time the bird crowed at midnight was to herald the day of Christ's birth. That connection was vividly presented to Emilia and me in a church in Puerto Rico, where a crèche was augmented by a live rooster in a cage behind the altar.

O COME, ALL YE FAITHFUL

✦

CRÈCHES IN TIME AND PLACE

Christians believe that God became human in the person of Christ. The crèches in the Govan family collection present wonderful examples of "God like us"—a human being in time and place for the purpose of our salvation. Just as God created us in His image, the artists of these crèches have each created God in their own image, interpreting the Christmas story in terms of their own cultural milieu.

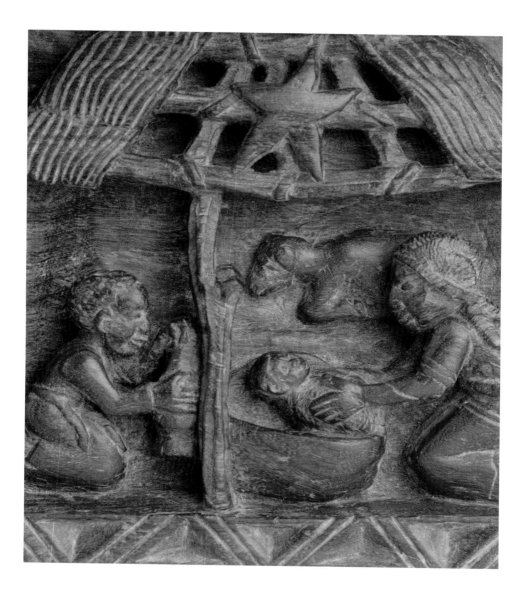

POLAND
✦
ANTONI KAMIŃSKI

A gift from one of our sons in 1999, this endearing work was acquired from Folk Arts of Poland, a shop in Santa Fe, New Mexico. The shop's owner, Gregory Quevillon, provided information about the carver, Antoni Kamiński (born 1947), who is self-taught. Kamiński's early works are simple, unpainted or stained and varnished pieces. His later carvings are complex scenes in three dimensions and bas-relief, containing up to five layers of figures and painted with watercolors. His subjects include folk tales, religious stories (including the Nativity), historical events, and rural scenes. Carving remained a hobby for Kamiński until 1978, when he gave up his job to commit to his craft after gaining national recognition.

This large crèche contains six groups of figures on a 3-foot (90-cm) base. The most striking is the single-piece

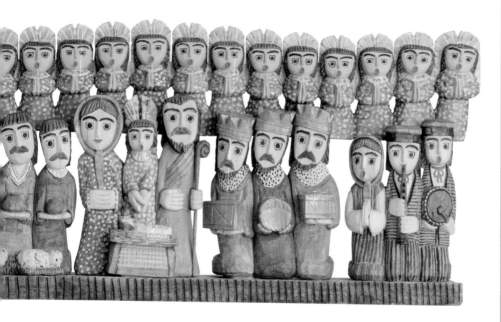

carving of a heavenly choir of seventeen angels heralding
the birth of Christ. Another angel joins the Holy Family,
and they are flanked by groupings of kings and shepherds,
all of whom bear gifts. Two groups of villagers, some with
musical instruments, accompany the angel chorus.

53

NEW ZEALAND
+
GEOFF PRYOR

New Zealand does not have a long tradition of crèche-making. As I searched for an example, I was put in touch with Geoff Pryor, who was enthusiastic to create one—his first—reflecting the Maori culture. Geoff was born in England and moved to New Zealand in 1952. This crèche came to me through the generosity of Geoff and others: the Infant's Maori cloak was made by Leone James and Hilary James; its motif was designed by Shirley Kelland; and Dr. Erlinda Punongbayan brought us the crèche.

Set in a box with three scenes to be viewed from the front, it focuses on Jesus, the only three-dimensional figure in the crèche, who is depicted at the back, arriving by *waka* (canoe) from a faraway land. Pryor sought to convey New Zealand's "remoteness . . . from the event." The second panel bears a painting of a woman's face with traditional Maori markings, representing Mary or the mother's spirit watching over her son. The front panel shows a forest scene,

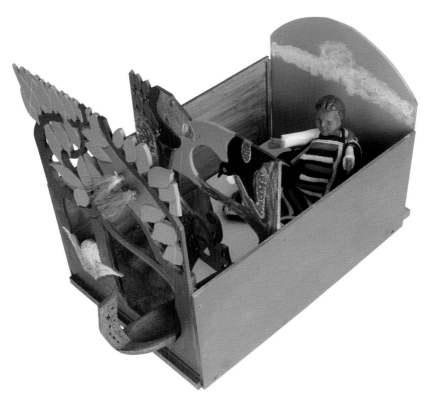

with the blossoms of the pohutakawa tree (the New Zealand Christmas tree). Despite my attempts to pay for the crèche, Geoff told me he wanted to present it as a gift— a touching final gesture to a touching experience.

EGYPT
✦
ABDOU ZEINHOUM

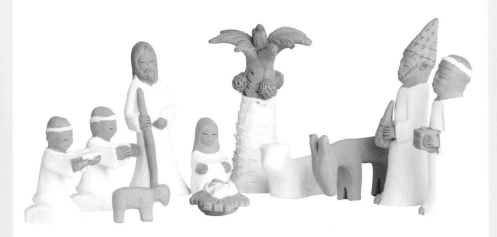

A bdou Zeinhoum is known for his delicate nativity
figures. He has practiced his pottery handicraft for
thirty years, living in old Cairo for most of that time, and
sells his crèches primarily to shops visited by tourists. The
figures and the finely detailed palm tree in this scene reflect
its Middle Eastern origin. The nativity was a gift from a
USAID colleague.

SWAZILAND
✦
ZAGARIAFUMO

The carver of this crèche lives in Swaziland, a small country bordering South Africa and Mozambique. The piece, signed simply "Zagariafumo," shows a traditional grouping in which the people are depicted as Africans. While this is common among the African crèches in the collection, the expressively carved figures make this indigenous portrayal particularly notable. Unusually for an African nativity, the wooden figures are painted rather than stained or polished.

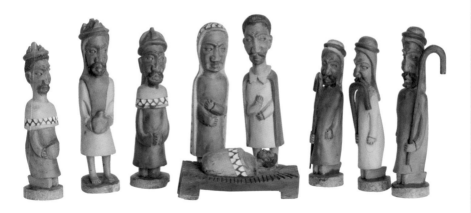

LITHUANIA

✦
VLADAS RAKUCKAS

Emilia and I especially wanted crèches that reflected our ancestral heritages. It was easy to acquire Italian examples, but many years of effort failed to find a Lithuanian crèche to reflect my heritage. Lithuania, the last European country to be converted to Christianity, has strong folk traditions in which wood carving plays an integral part, but it endured years of Communist prohibition of religious expression.

Finally, the American–Lithuanian owner of a Baltic goods shop in Boston told me that he had arranged for a Lithuanian sculptor to come to Florida for three weeks to work on a project for an American–Lithuanian community in Florida. The sculptor, Vladas Rakuckas (born 1956) studied computer programming but began carving at the age of twenty-four. I was told he would make a crèche on commission during his stay, despite never having created one before. Elated, I asked that he include a Lithuanian folk-art motif.

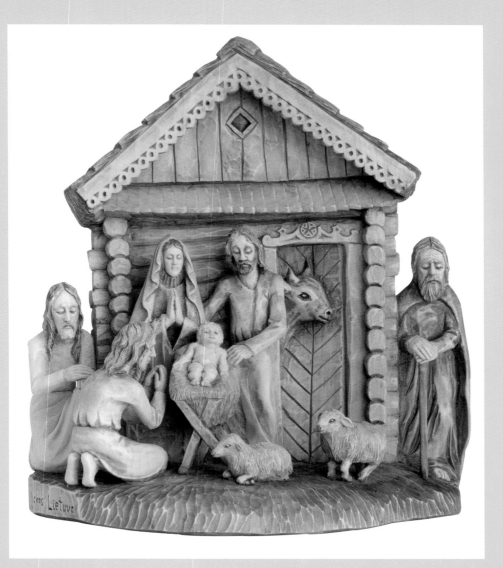

Rakuckas carved the crèche during his evenings, sometimes working all night, and we were thrilled to meet him when he unexpectedly stopped at our home in Virginia, en route back to Lithuania, to present us with the carving. He created a stunning work from a single piece of tree trunk (previous page). The Lithuanian motifs I requested are on the eaves and above the door of the stable, and the cow poking its head through the door offers a humorous touch.

Once home, Rakuckas decided to make himself a crèche. He exhibited it in Vilnius, and a German merchant persuaded him to produce similar ones to be sold in Germany. Early in 1993, Rakuckas sold me the second crèche, the only one still in his possession: "I think that the best place for it is among your collection." He confessed to finding carving these crèches an all-consuming effort, and wanted to broaden his work. On seeing the meticulous carving of the second crèche, I understood why. This intricate scene (opposite), created from a single block of linden wood, is set in an exceptionally detailed grove of trees, a context that symbolizes the Lithuanian love of forests that predates the Christian era, and recalls St. Francis's outdoor celebration in 1223.

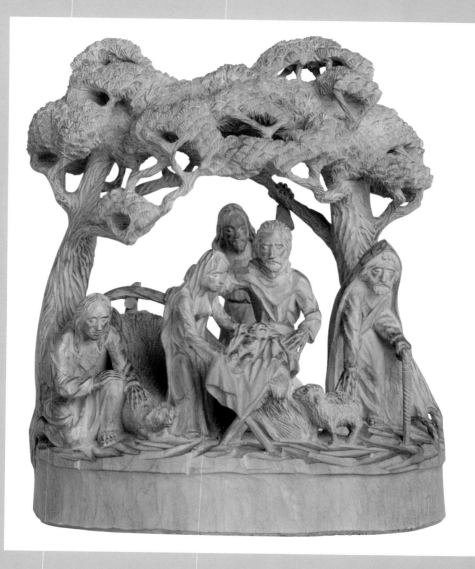

SWEDEN
✦
CHARLOTTE WEIBULL

Preserving Swedish traditions by making dolls wearing folk costumes has been a passion for Charlotte Weibull (born 1917) for more than fifty years, and an interest her family has shared for two centuries. The folk center she founded—Möllegården, in Åkarp—houses a museum, exhibition hall, and doll workshop, among other facilities. Weibull documents Sweden's folk costumes by creating dolls in traditional dress. She created the nation's current folk costume, which Queen Silvia wears on Sweden's National Day.

The museum holds Weibull's collection of more than 200 crèches from around the world. Her interest was stimulated in 1958 by a visit to Poland, where she was

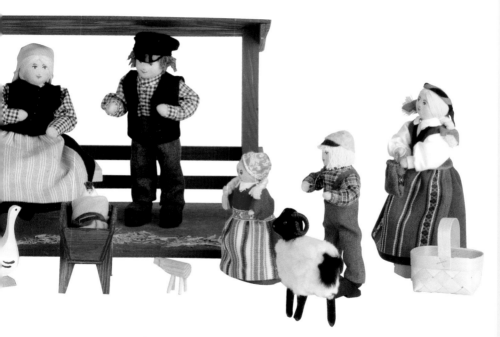

impressed by crèches reflecting Polish heritage. Weibull has designed two crèches, both of which are made in her workshop. One is a traditional nativity. The other (shown here) is a colorful scene, with people dressed in folk costumes of the province of Scania, where she was born.

MALAWI
✦
DENIS MOYO

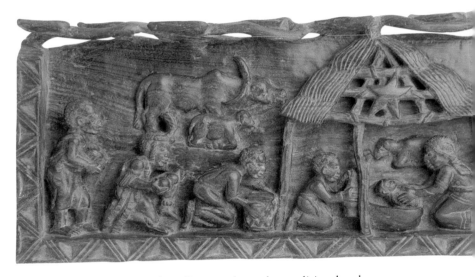

Malawian crèches illustrate how the tradition has been adapted in Africa. When we visited in 1989, Emilia and I could not find any crèches. However, a year later, we received as gifts two beautiful Malawian artworks from USAID friends, one bought there (see pages 174–75), the

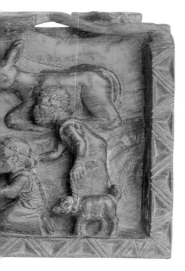

other—the relief carving featured here—commissioned for us. Denis Moyo (born 1976) was then training at the Catholic KuNgoni Center of Culture and Art in Mua, founded in 1976 by Father Claude Boucher to promote Malawi's "awareness of its own culture" and contribute to the "expression of the Christian message." Renowned for excellent craftsmanship, the center has produced works for individuals and churches throughout Europe, including the Vatican.

In this charming depiction, the stable has a star in the roof and Mary tends the Baby Jesus. It is one of the very few crèches in the collection in which Mary is not in the traditional pose of either holding or watching the Infant.

ROBED IN GLORY

✦

COSTUMES

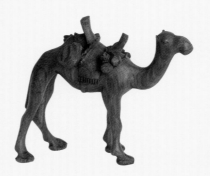

Certain costumes evoke certain cultures, and the costumes worn by a crèche's figures often reveal the provenance of the scene and sometimes its historical period. Much can be inferred from the artist's use of costume: social status, occupation, and, on occasion, religion.

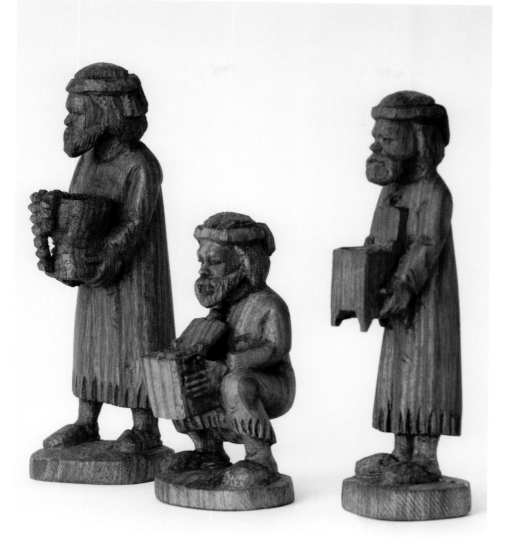

ECUADOR
✦
MICHAEL AYALA

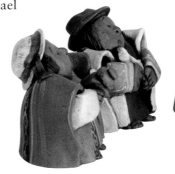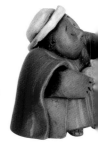

Ecuadorian artist Michael Ayala explains, "Many nativities I have seen in my country don't represent the native people very much; some even have blond and blue-eyed characters in the Holy Family. So I decided to design something very Ecuadorian and to represent the different ethnic groups in my country." Primarily a painter, Ayala taught himself to work with clay around 1991, and depicts Ecuadorian themes—especially popular festivities, including the Nativity. He was inspired to create crèches by childhood experiences: he remembers visiting many houses where each family "tried to have the biggest and most beautiful nativity."

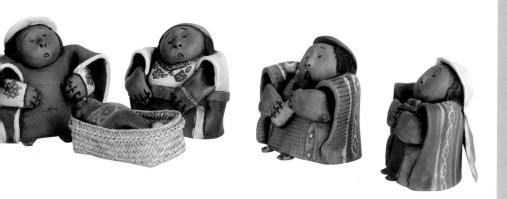

The figures' clothing in this hand-made terra-cotta crèche represents different regions of Ecuador. The Holy Family wears the dress of the Otavalo region. An angel, with a panpipe, represents Cañar. A shepherd with a hen represents Salasaca; one with a pig, Tungurahua; and one with a guinea pig (*cuy*), Cotopaxi. Another shepherd represents Otavalo and plays a *bocina*, an Andean horn.

ETHIOPIA
✦
HANNAH LÜTHI/
LISTEWORK ATNAFU

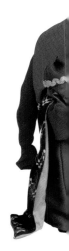

This attractive nativity was made by individuals supported by the Signum Vitae Project, founded in 1989 by Hanni Lüthi (a former arts and crafts teacher), her husband, and a team of volunteers to provide vocational training and employment for disabled people. Lüthi designed the nativity, and Listework Atnafu, who is disabled, produced the figures. A fellow artisan created the wood portions of the crèche.

Most Christians in Ethiopia belong to the Ethiopian Orthodox Church, and the primary artistic expression of their religion is through painted icons. The indigenous presentation of this more unusual three-dimensional nativity is very appealing: Mary wears a *netela* (shawl), Joseph holds a *djira* (flyswatter), and Jesus lies in a stone manger of a kind often used for feeding cattle. Indeed, some scholars say that the Infant would have been laid in a stone manger, not the wooden one commonly depicted. The figures

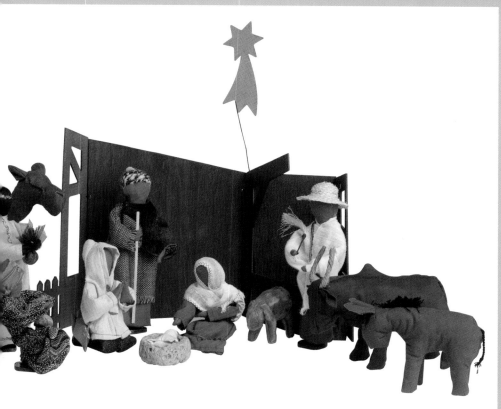

are clothed in fabric. The standing shepherd represents the people of the Ethiopian highlands, while the kneeling, hooded figure represents the younger generation, who increasingly wear Western clothes.

KOREA
✦
BOO HO KIM

The beautifully rendered costumes in this nativity evoke exotic silks but were, in fact, crafted from linden wood by a master carver. In 1961, as a young man in his twenties, Boo Ho Kim started a wood-carving business in Seoul. He considers himself self-taught, yet became a teacher of teachers, demonstrating the technical and practical aspects of his craft for fine-arts instructors.

Kim, a Catholic, began making nativities in 1965, when a foreigner asked him for a Western-style example. He saw a new market for his carvings and was among the first Koreans to produce this type of work, later also making Korean-style scenes. He does not consider himself as famous, carving to earn "his bread," as he says. He retired in the early 1990s to a small farm, and now carves as a hobby, especially liking to make toys for his grandchildren.

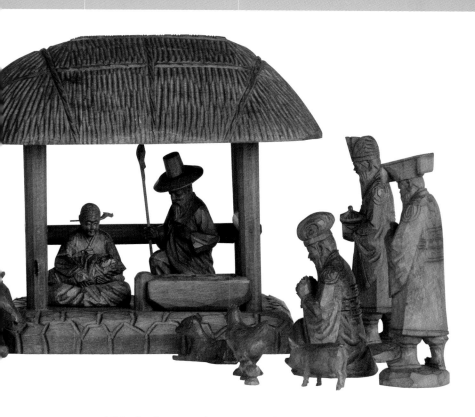

This finely carved nativity reflects the style of sixteenth-century Korea. Mary cradles the Infant as she sits in a small, straw-thatched farm structure. The kings wear stately garb typical of the Chosun Dynasty.

THAILAND

✦

KHUNYING TONGKORN CHANDAVIMOL

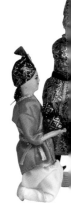

What is a doll without costumes? It is not surprising that this crèche from Thailand's master doll-maker includes remarkable clothes.

In 1955, impressed on a visit to Japan by its doll-making tradition, Tongkorn Chandavimol attended a short doll-making course in Tokyo. When she returned home, she started making dolls in traditional Thai costumes, set up a workshop, Bangkok Dolls (which employs about twenty people), and soon gained an international reputation. In the 1960s, the government gave her the title *Khunying* (similar to "Lady" in Britain) for her contribution to Thai culture. Thai royalty has presented her dolls to several world leaders, and her workshop made a doll of Pope John Paul II for a Christian group to present to the pontiff when he visited Thailand.

A Buddhist who attended a Presbyterian school, Khunying Tongkorn began making nativities in the 1990s. Here, the

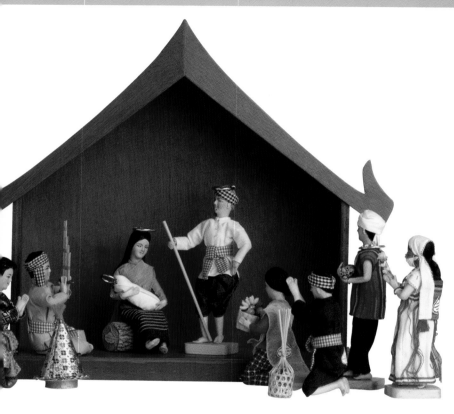

Holy Family is presented in contemporary Thai dress; the common people are dressed as Karen farmers. The kings wear silk: one is dressed as a Thai nobleman, another as a Chinese mandarin, and the third as an Indian prince.

MALI
✦
HASSA PASCAL
MOUNKORO

Hassa Pascal Mounkoro is a Catholic who enjoys making crèches as "a sort of evangelization, a way to talk about my love for Jesus." Born in 1968 into an animist family, he lives in the capital of Mali, Bamako. He was considered a master carver at the age of twenty-four, and he began training several other carvers, who have gone on to establish their own workshops.

Mounkoro specializes in nativities, which are rare in Mali, a predominately Muslim country. He began to make them after accepting a request from a Norwegian missionary, who gave him a book containing nativity scenes from which he has derived ideas.

76

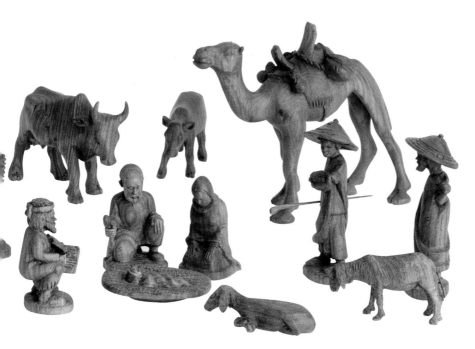

Mounkoro's considerable talent is evident in the finely detailed figures, which display indigenous characteristics. The shepherds wear the round, pointed hats customary for the Fulani herders in the region.

ARIZONA, USA
✦
JENI BABIN

Not all costume inspiration comes from clothing: the intricate design on the figures' dress in this crèche was inspired by the rose window of Chartres Cathedral in France. New Orleans-born Jeni Babin, who lives in Arizona, is known for her sculptural stoneware. Initially she drew and painted, but she began working with clay in the early 1980s. Since then, she says, "I just couldn't do anything else. Clay simply sings to my spirit." Babin studied with Japanese masters for three years and spent ten years developing her style. She is not sure, however, how to describe it: "Robust contemporary with traditional overtones? I like to merge past and present into a contemporary artifact." Here, she achieves this mixture by incorporating the stained-glass design. All her crèches have been in one piece. She says, "I put a lot of love into my pieces and feel that they are a way of . . . connecting with people."

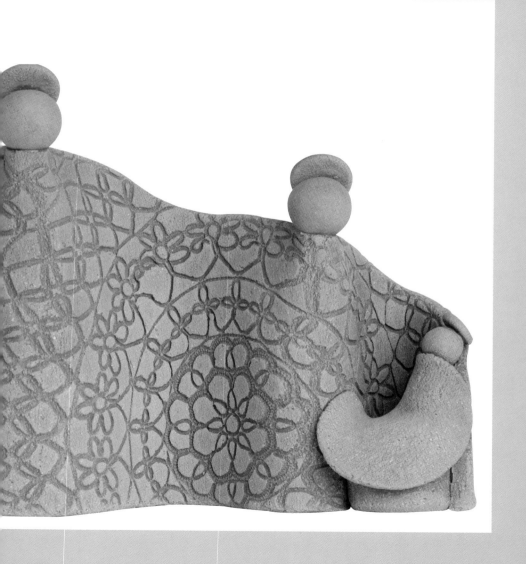

HEAVEN & NATURE ABOUND

✦

FLORA AND FAUNA

It surprises some to learn that the only animals mentioned in the Gospel accounts of Christ's birth are the shepherds' flock. Animals abound in artists' renderings and retellings of the Nativity on account of a key element of the story: the manger into which the newborn Christ was laid. Conjecture, Old Testament prophesies, and legends have all contributed to the menagerie that sometimes surrounds the Baby Jesus in crèche scenes. As the tradition has been interpreted around the world, animals—like costumes, plants, and flowers—have become another medium for indigenous adaptation. This earthly abundance joins Heaven's angels and star in celebrating the event.

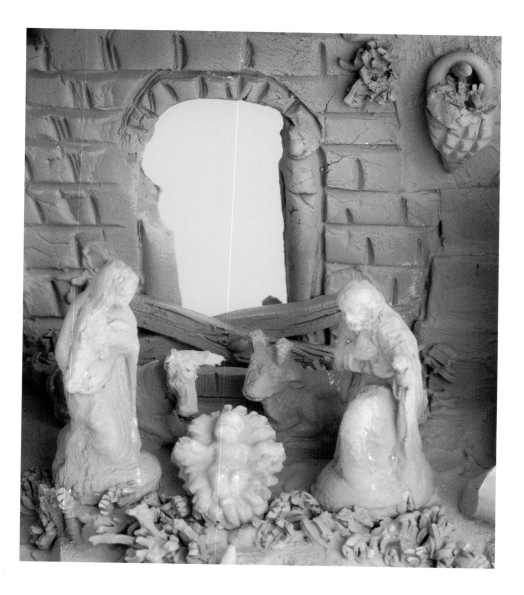

MEXICO

✦

UNKNOWN ARTIST

This intriguing nativity presentation is set on a rounded ceramic base. The heavenly star rises above the assembly of angel, shepherd, kings, animals, and the Holy Family. There is a plant to one side. A bird—perhaps a dove representing the Holy Spirit—alights on one edge, while a rooster appears on the other. As well as the expected cow, donkey, and sheep, a goat appears. Emilia and I acquired this piece in Guadalajara, but there was no information about its origin.

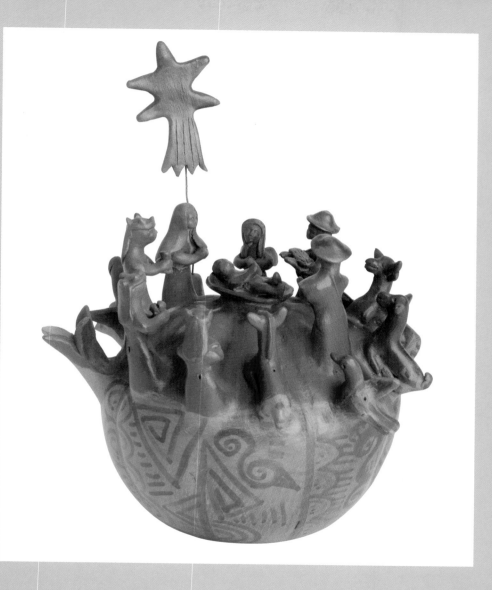

MALTA
✦
JOSEPH CAMILLERI

A n avid promoter in Malta of the nativity tradition, Joseph Camilleri (born 1943) is known for his fine work with clay. He enjoyed making figures as a boy, but started working as a serious ceramist only when he was thirty years old. He learned some techniques from other potters, but is mostly self-taught.

Camilleri was inspired to create and exhibit his first crèche, which was sculpted

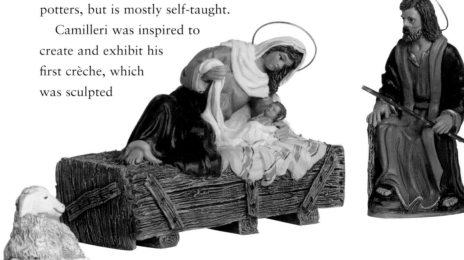

using toothpicks, after attending the international congress of crèche societies held in Madrid in 1992. His nativity was praised locally, and he has devoted himself to crèche art ever since. He uses no molds: all figures are individually made. He creates delicate bas-reliefs as well as colorful three-dimensional presentations, and considers his style a traditional one reflecting the Bethlehem of Christ's time, not one typical of Maltese traditions. Camilleri teaches the art of "crib-making," lectures, and is active in his local nativity society.

In this scene, which was commissioned for the collection, the customary grouping of cow, donkey, and sheep attends the birth of the Infant. Mary reclines, as she so often does in the Eastern iconographic tradition; unusually, Joseph is depicted sitting.

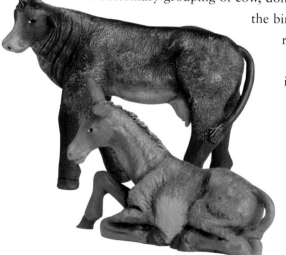

ITALY
+
UNKNOWN ARTIST

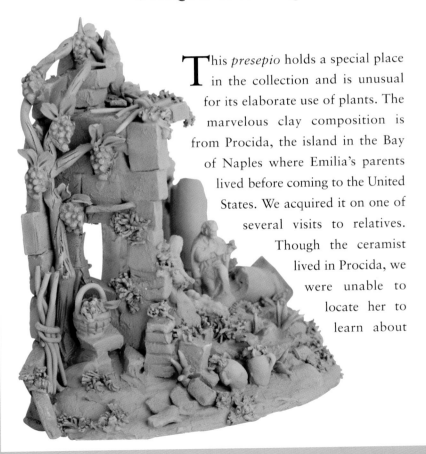

This *presepio* holds a special place in the collection and is unusual for its elaborate use of plants. The marvelous clay composition is from Procida, the island in the Bay of Naples where Emilia's parents lived before coming to the United States. We acquired it on one of several visits to relatives. Though the ceramist lived in Procida, we were unable to locate her to learn about her and her work. This fragile clay scene is filled with tiny details of plants, flowers, and jars. A basket of grapes sits at one side. The broken column, a common element in Neapolitan *presepi*, is often interpreted as symbolizing the fall of the Roman Empire and the rise of Christianity.

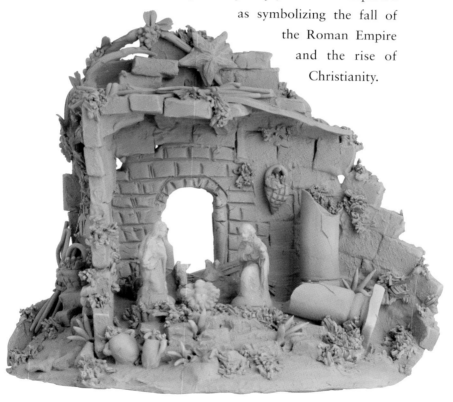

BRAZIL

CARMÉLIA RODRIGUES
DA SILVA

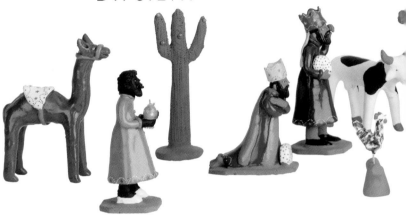

A gift from one of our sons, this crèche from Alto do Mauro in northeastern Brazil includes a rooster and cacti. The small village and its neighboring city, Caruaru, are considered by UNESCO to be the most important centers for figurative art in the Americas. Clay figurines, which became traditional in the region, were first created by Master Vitalino Pereira dos Santos (died 1963). His style inspired local artisans to make similar figurines, and the

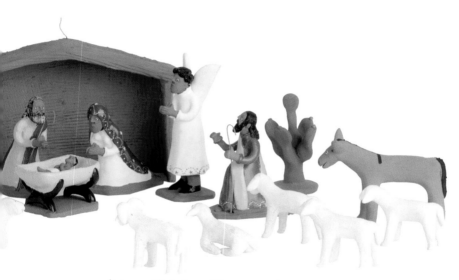

tradition still thrives. There are about two hundred artisans in Alto do Mauro, most of whom work in Vitalino's style.

Carmélia Rodrigues da Silva has worked with clay since she was seven. She learned from her father, who she says was "one of the first disciples of Master Vitalino." Rodrigues's mother, children, and other relatives also make clay figures. This brightly hand-painted crèche is very much in Vitalino's style. As in many Hispanic crèches, the rooster is prominent.

PUERTO RICO
✦
JUAN CRUZ AVILÉS

Emilia and I visited Puerto Rico in 1991, and looked for a crèche by a native *santero*. We did not meet any *santeros*, but noted several whose carvings were in our hotel shop. Once home, I wrote to one of them, Juan Cruz Avilés, who within a couple of weeks sent an unpainted crèche and promised the painted one we had requested (seen here).

Cruz (born 1919) lives in Lares, western Puerto Rico, where he was raised by his grandparents. At fourteen, he dreamed that he should begin carving and restore *santos* to help with school expenses. Skeptical, he told his grandmother, who forbade him to touch her *santos*. When she relented, Cruz began to restore and carve them, without any training. He believes his skill was given to him to solve a problem. He carved his first crèche around 1945, and, since retiring from the town administration, has dedicated himself to carving.

This crèche reflects Cruz's simple, primitive style, with boldly colored figures against the stable's white interior.

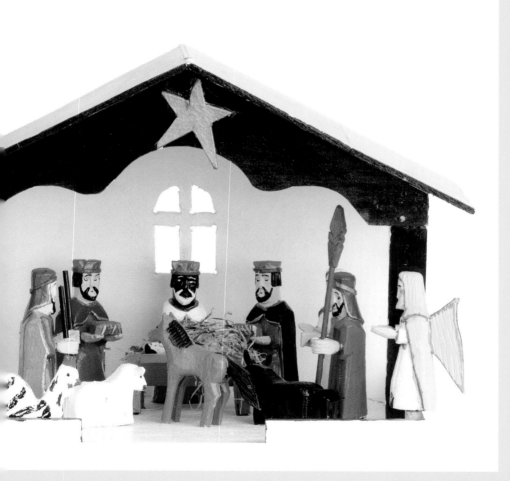

PERU

VICTOR FAUSTINO CHÁVEZ QUISPE

Born in Lima in 1966, Victor Chávez faced a number of hardships as he grew up. He worked at menial jobs from an early age to help his mother support the family. As a teenager, Chávez went to live with his grandmother in Quinua, where he began to make ceramics. Unable to pay for classes, he had no formal training, but was taught various techniques by local artisans. Once he gained recognition for his work, he returned to Lima, where he eventually taught ceramics for an organization directed by a Spanish priest.

This nativity was commissioned for the collection and is set in the Andean highlands, complete with cacti. Nature's bounty is also represented by the gift of food in a bowl, which includes cactus fruit and *cuy* (guinea pig). The Christ Child, angel, and shepherd wear the *chullo*, a traditional hat. Chávez's artistic skill is evident in the figures' delicately defined features and the finely detailed decoration of their clothing.

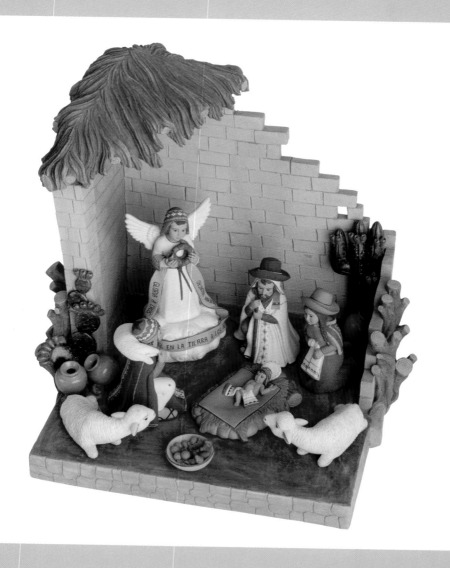

CALIFORNIA, USA
✦
CHRISTOPHER MAYA

Christopher Maya was exposed to devotional art as a youth, in his family home. Born in El Paso, Texas, in 1961, he now lives in California. He began to carve in the mid-1990s and is dedicated to making *santos* and holy images; he also paints and makes woodblock prints. He says he creates "as a devotion." In this nativity, carved in the Spanish Colonial style, Joseph is a commanding figure, but the artist's focus is on the donkey, or *burro*. Maya feels that the *burro* is "undercredited in the Nativity story," and as animals give "love unconditionally"—in this instance to the Christ Child—they are the real stars of the Nativity tale.

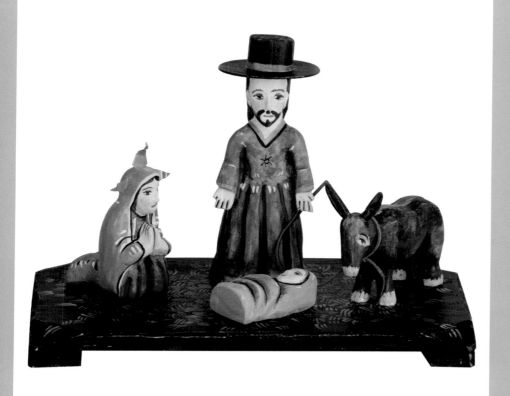

LIBERIA
✦
UNKNOWN ARTIST

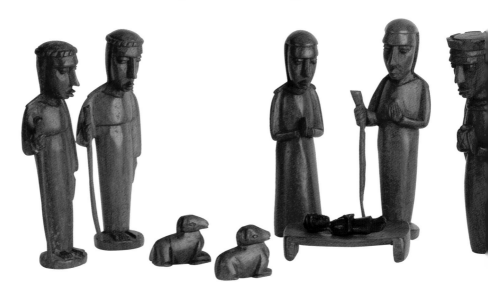

Some elements of the Nativity story, such as the camels on which the magi traveled, are embellishments, but for many they have become essential to the tale. Crafted from red wood, this crèche projects a warmth, especially in the

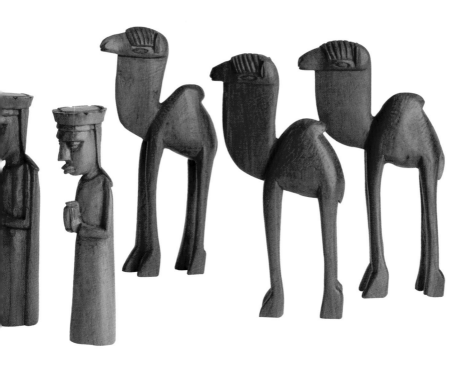

appealing camel figures. It was commissioned as a gift for the collection by a USAID friend who was working in Monrovia at the time, and was carved by skilled Liberian artisans who occupied a roadside stall opposite my friend's office.

KENYA
+
UNKNOWN ARTIST

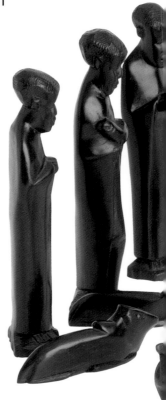

This crèche is probably the only nativity in the world in which most of the animal characters are warthogs. It was commissioned for me by my staff at USAID. They entrusted an agency employee in Nairobi to find a carver, and presented the nativity to me on my retirement after thirty-four years with the agency. My staff had asked for warthogs to be included because of my fondness for them, and in remembrance of a stuffed toy warthog we named Wally that was the gift of a former staffer and had been the office's mascot for a decade. Unfortunately, the name of the carver who created this warthog nativity is not known.

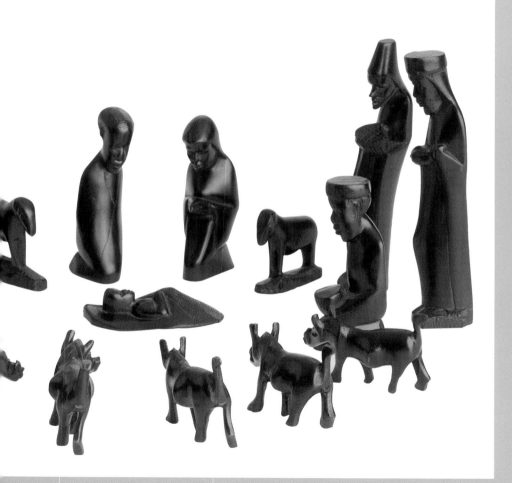

BULGARIA
✦
TRAYAN GABROVSKI

Sheep are often considered essential in crèche scenes because of Luke's mention of the shepherds' flock. In this scene, two sheep are beside the shepherd who, startled, shields his face at the appearance of the angel, who has come to proclaim the good news of Christ's birth. This portrayal of the shepherd is unique in the collection.

Trayan Gabrovski, born in 1950 in a northern village, now lives in Teteven in central Bulgaria. Since the age of thirty he has made his living as a wood-carver. He says that he did not learn his craft in a school, "but it might be God's blessing for me." Gabrovski carves reliefs as well as three-dimensional pieces, and his works include both religious and secular themes. This softly colored crèche was commissioned for the collection.

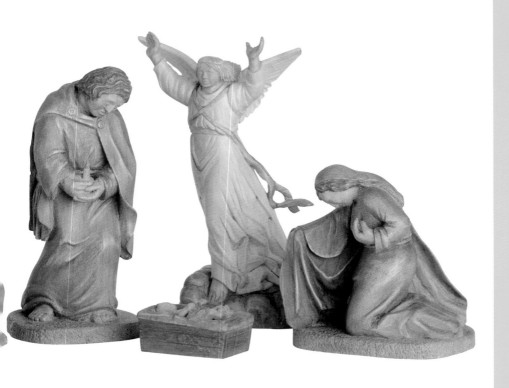

NEW MEXICO, USA
SABINITA LÓPEZ ORTIZ

The *santero* José Dolores López of Cordóva helped revive interest in Spanish Colonial carving in the early twentieth century, and his descendants continue to carve in the "Cordóva style." Among them are his grandchildren Sabinita López Ortiz and Eluid Levi Martínez, both of whose work is represented in the collection (see also pages 246–47).

Sabinita (born 1938) was adopted by her uncle, George López, and his wife, Silvanita, who were childless. She began to carve when still a child, under George's guidance. After she married, she taught her husband to carve, and they shared a workshop with George and Silvanita for some years. The family tradition continues with Sabinita's children.

Sabinita, who has gained recognition for her work, describes her carving as "the same as my father and grandfather." This crèche is carved from aspen and cedar, and incorporates elements of the family style, including curved branches (the *coronita*), leaves, and a bird.

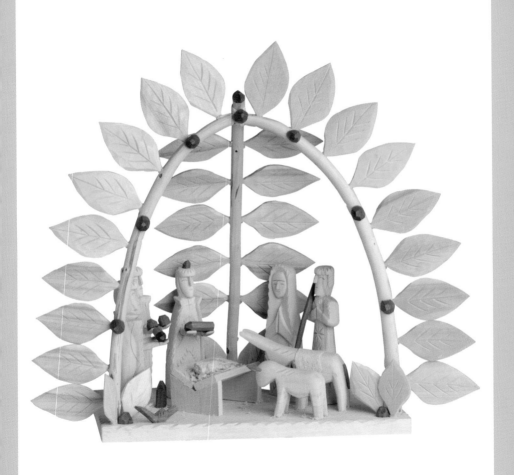

A JOYFUL NOISE

✦

MUSICAL EXPRESSIONS

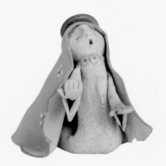

Music has become an integral part of Christmas traditions around the world. Each world culture has its unique form of musical expression—particular musical instruments, dances, and songs—so it is not surprising that a diverse range of musical genres can be found represented in crèche scenes.

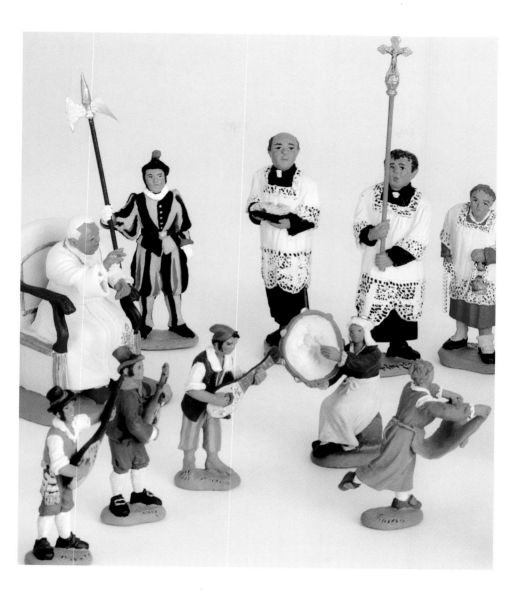

GHANA
✦
MOHAMMED AMIN

Musical expression abounds in this crèche from Ghana. Mohammed Amin (born 1968) is a self-taught potter who devotes his skills to honoring Ghanaian culture and customs, especially those of northern Ghana, where he lives. A Muslim married to a Catholic, Amin taught at the Tamale Institute of Cross-Cultural Studies, and now has his own ceramics workshop.

Amin's crèches are steeped in the culture of the region. In this scene, he presents the Holy Family as Dagomba, his own tribe. Drums are especially important to the community, being a source of entertainment as well as communication. Here, the drummer announces Christ's birth and summons all. The xylophonist is a Dagaties tribesman, the flutist a

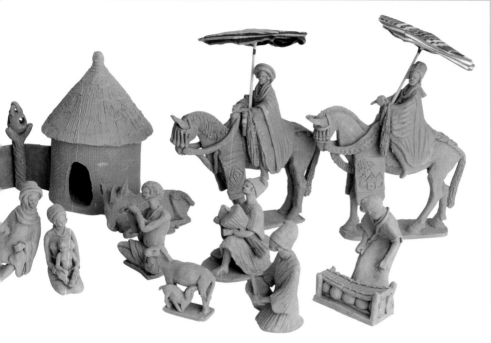

Kasina; both instruments are important in ceremonies and festivals. The kings—only two—represent the Dagomba and Gonja chiefs, their importance signified by the size of the umbrellas and the horses' lavish adornment. When Amin includes a third king in his crèches, he is portrayed as a nomadic Tuareg, riding a camel. In the background are huts of the style used in northern Ghana to house animals.

CZECH REPUBLIC
JAN VOKOUN

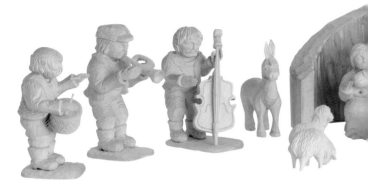

Many Czech nativities include musicians, not surprisingly given the Czechs' great love of music. This piece is by artist Jan Vokoun, who was born in 1956 and began carving when he was about forty. Vokoun is self-taught, but feels that working with wood is in his family, since his grandfather was a carpenter. His first carvings included crèches, which he continues to make, and he also enjoys making marionettes, especially figures of local villagers as musicians.

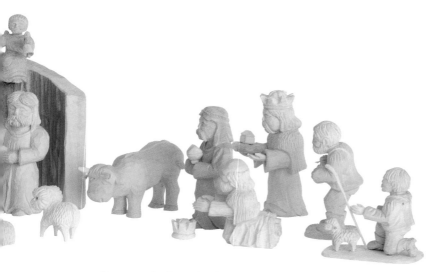

I commissioned this crèche when I met Vokoun demonstrating his craft at a museum in his town, Třebechovice pod Orebem. He invited me to his home studio, where we discussed the kind of nativity he would make. The resulting scene reflects his style, which he says is in the folk-art tradition of the region. Mary holds the Infant while a merry trio of musicians serenades him. The shepherds and kings gather in adoration while the angel rings a bell, perhaps to accompany the musical trio.

ITALY
·
ALBERTO FINIZIO

T his piece evokes music both festive and sacred. The people dance to celebrate Christ's birth; the Pope blesses the assemblage; and a Eucharistic procession takes place. To many Christians, the Eucharist symbolizes Christ's presence in the world. This clay crèche was commissioned for the collection with the specific request for a figure of the then pontiff, John Paul II.

Alberto Finizio (born 1956) began to make nativities as a child, and is self-taught, although he has learned much from artists in the Associazione Italiana Amici del Presepio (Italian Association of Friends of the Crèche), in which he is active. In the Italian tradition, he also makes detailed background settings for his nativities. His style is traditional, but he strives for original

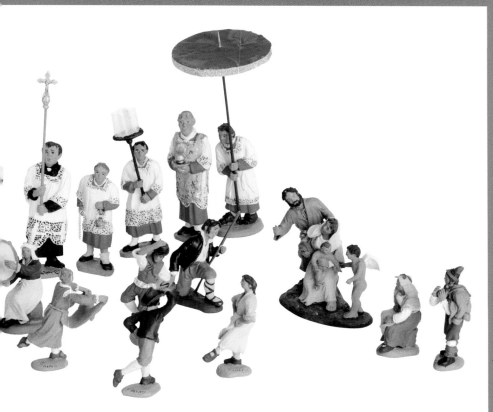

presentations. In this scene, the people are in nineteenth-century Roman dress. Finizio says that for him "the nativity scene is . . . a message of love and brotherhood, a passion that occupies a great deal of my time."

NEW MEXICO, USA
JIL GURULÉ

This nativity was commissioned for the collection with the specific request that mariachi figures be included. Mariachi music, along with a style of dress, originated in the Mexican state of Jalisco. Jil Gurulé, a New Orleans native who now lives in New Mexico, creates expressive crèches with bold colors stemming from her work as a painter (see also pages 266–67). She has worked with clay since 1977, and is self-taught. She feels drawn to the "quiet dignity and beauty" of the native peoples of New Mexico, especially northern New Mexico, and enjoys creating pieces for the Native American market. Gurulé also makes saint figures to sell at Santa Fe's annual Spanish Market, and collectors seek her Santa Claus figures.

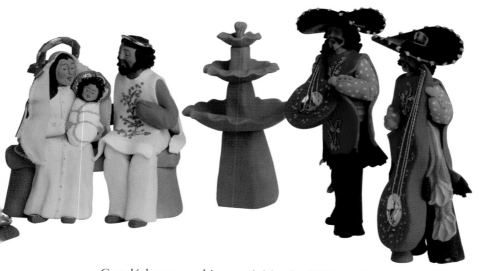

Gurulé began making nativities in 1984, and creates a new presentation every year. She does not use molds. Asked why she is attracted to the theme, Gurulé replies that crèches are "peaceful" and that the Nativity "is a beautiful, hopeful story."

In this scene, some of the musicians perform for the Christ Child while others offer their instruments as gifts. The Holy Family is placed on a bench as if sitting in a Spanish square or park.

VIRGINIA, USA
CAROLINE TAIT

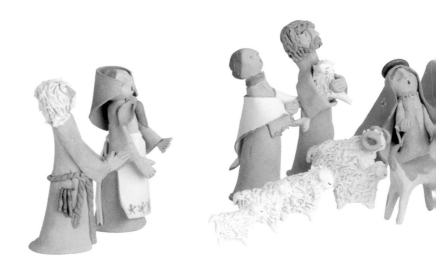

This joyful clay scene was created by Caroline Tait, an artist who was living in Virginia at the time we acquired it. The figures all seem to be honoring the Christ Child with song, led by Mary and Joseph. The Christ Child

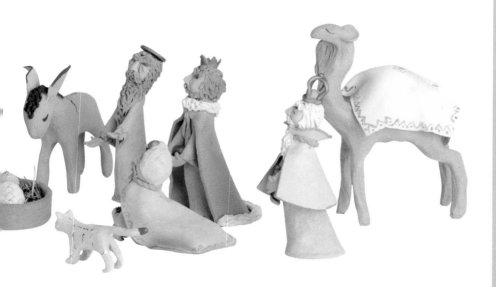

lies comfortably in swaddling clothes. The innkeeper, keys
at his side, and his wife join the kings and shepherds. A dog
and a cat complete the scene. Tait has created similarly
delightful scenes of Noah's Ark.

CZECH REPUBLIC
✦
PAVEL MATUŠKA

LISTEN III

This piece includes a *shofar*, a horn traditionally used to announce important Jewish events. This juxtaposition might be expected from Pavel Matuška, whose portrayals are unconventional, often humorous. Born in Třebechovice pod Orebem, where he still lives, in 1944, he trained as a graphic designer, but is a self-taught cartoonist, painter, and carver. He did not start carving until 1998, and has made only a few nativities. In this scene, he eschews the traditional stable with an ox and donkey, choosing instead a "neutral" background of columns and angels spreading the news. Although humor is a hallmark of his work, this crèche is foreboding. While Joseph holds the Infant aloft and Mary beckons all to greet him, the armed Roman soldier with a bag of silver symbolizes Christ's betrayal and violent fate. Matuška says: "No one is paying attention to the soldier; only a little dog senses something ominous." Jesus's extended arms foreshadow his death on the cross.

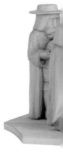

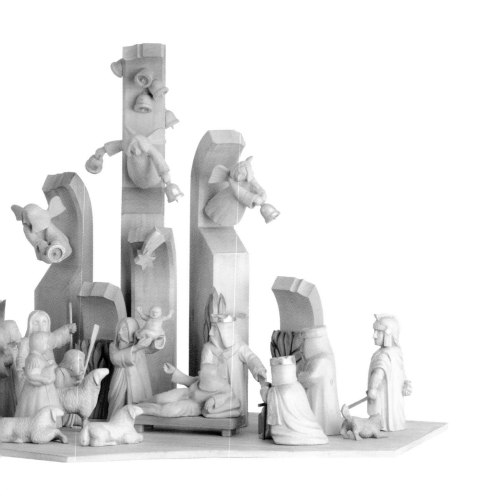

GiFTS OF THE mAGi

✦

EXPRESSiONS OF HOmAGE

Anyone familiar with the Christmas story can name the gifts that the magi presented to the Baby Jesus, but few can interpret their significance. Although the gifts' profundity is often forgotten, their value and the determination of the magi to make their presentation are remembered through the celebrations of gift-giving at Christmas and Epiphany. Gold, frankincense, and myrrh have powerful associations in Western culture, but the solemnity of the gifts can also be expressed in valuables and materials that are sacred to other cultures around the world.

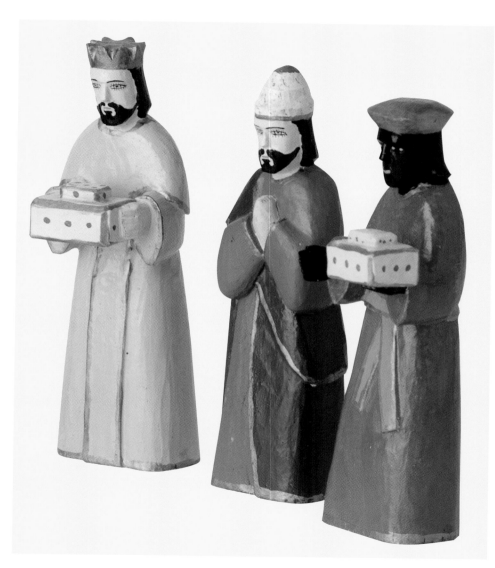

BURKINA FASO
✦
UNKNOWN ARTIST

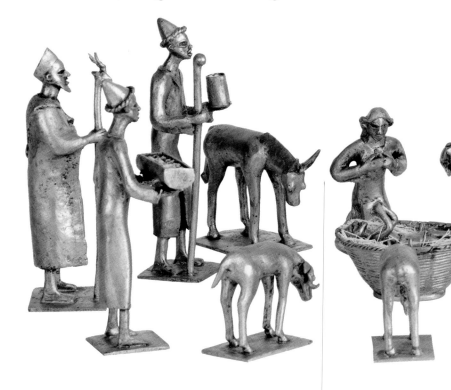

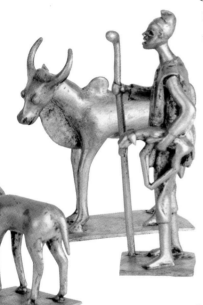

One of the reasons this crèche from Burkina Faso is such a favorite is the wonderful portrayal of the kings and their unique gifts. Burkina Faso, a former French colony in West Africa, is a largely Muslim country with a Christian presence. This striking bronze crèche was commissioned for the collection through a USAID colleague, and was made by a group of artisans in Ouagadougou, the capital city of this poor Sahelian country. The pieces are each signed and were probably made by artisans at the Centre National d'Artisanat d'Art. The crèche figures are in Burkinabe dress. The kings merit special attention: two of them bear gifts of real grain, most likely sorghum and millet, while the third, bearded and regal, holds a staff topped by an animal's head, which is very finely sculpted. The indigenous animals bow in adoration to the Christ Child.

PARAGUAY
✦
RODRÍGUEZ

This crèche is signed "Rodríguez," perhaps by the woman carver Juana de Rodríguez. The style of the figures, all carved from a lightweight wood, suggests that the carver may have been from around Tobati, which has long been a center for crafts. The tradition of carving in Paraguay—especially of religious themes—dates to the Jesuits, who arrived in the

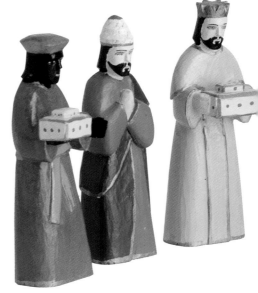

seventeenth century. Figures of saints (*santos*) have always been among the most popular carvings of the Tobati artisans. Joseph holds a lily, an allusion to the story of his

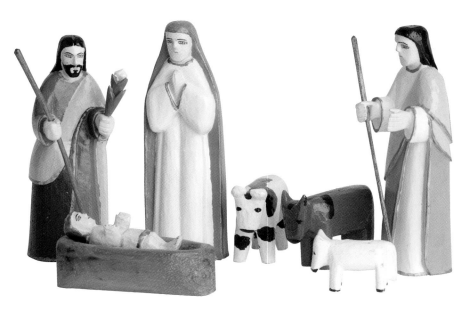

staff bursting into bloom as he became Mary's husband, sometimes interpreted as a symbol of purity. Two kings hold gifts of treasure boxes; the third holds his hands together, suggesting that his gift may be prayer.

MALAWI
✦
SUWEDI BIGULA

Suwedi Bigula, the carver of these three kings, which form part of an expressive crèche (see pages 174–75), is from the Yao tribe, and was born in 1951 in the village of Mwachumu in the Zomba district of southern Malawi. In the 1970s, Bigula received support from Catholic missionaries, who inspired him to carve on Christian themes. He began working at the KuNgoni Center of Culture and Art in Mua in 1983, and became one of the master carvers.

Bigula's crèche, carved from mlamba wood, conveys feelings of warmth and piety. The magi embody nobility and wisdom, and represent three proud tribal peoples of Malawi: the Yao king sits with legs outstretched and offers a gift of ivory; the Ngoni king, a chieftain with a feather headdress, offers a chicken; and the other king, representing the Chewa, offers a gourd containing medicine for the Child.

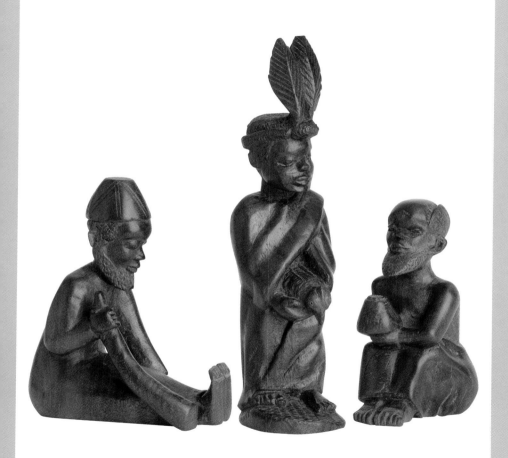

PUERTO RICO
JERRY SAINT GERMAIN

In this scene, the three kings, who are especially honored in Puerto Rico, pay homage to the Christ Child. According to the ceramist's widow, Leticia Saint Germain, the scene signifies the new beginning for humankind brought about by Christ's birth—a gift for all humanity. The boatlike setting, which evokes Noah's Ark, reinforces this theme.

Jerry Saint Germain was an architect and sculptor who also taught. Born in 1933 in Detroit, he moved to Puerto Rico in 1972. A few years later, he established a ceramics studio in San Juan. He devoted himself to sculpting and other art, such as murals, until his death in 1990. His work is somewhat abstract—as reflected in this nativity, which was a gift to me from a friend.

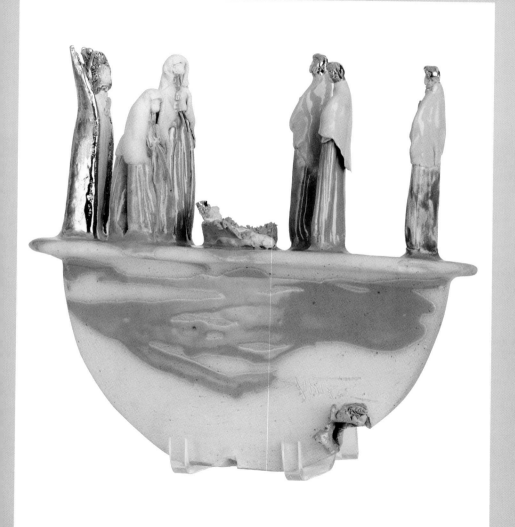

TOGO
✦
ROGER BAWI

R ather than three kings, two local leaders adore Jesus in this crèche of acacia wood. One, in hat and cloak of goatskin, is a *tchodjo*, a traditional priest from northern Togo. He is present to bless the event. The other, a chief in a royal hat, offers a box of gold. Two shepherds humbly hold their hats. One carries a sheep, the other a calabash, a gourd containing milk.

This charming scene was acquired through contacts at a Midwestern Benedictine monastery, who, in turn, contacted a Benedictine monastery in Togo. A brother at the African monastery was aware of a young carver, Roger Bawi, whom he asked to make a crèche for me.

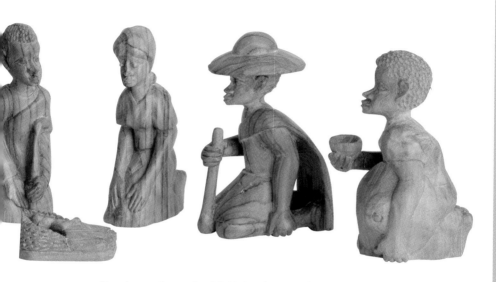

Bawi was born in 1960 in the northern town of Lassa-Algalade. He learned to carve while working with a Catholic missionary center in southern Togo, and began his own career as a wood sculptor in 1986, occasionally working with a Catholic mission in the town of Saoude, where he lives. In addition to crèches, he also makes such major church elements as altars, and other carvings.

TRADITION
& INNOVATION
✦
CREATING CRÈCHES

The materials and methods used in creating crèches are as varied as the people who produce them. Presented here is a selection of crèches made of varying materials—from the usual, such as clay and wood, to the unusual, such as potato clay and cinnamon paste. The techniques used in creating these wonderful scenes are equally diverse, and each crèche is a tribute to its creator's ingenuity, imagination, and skill.

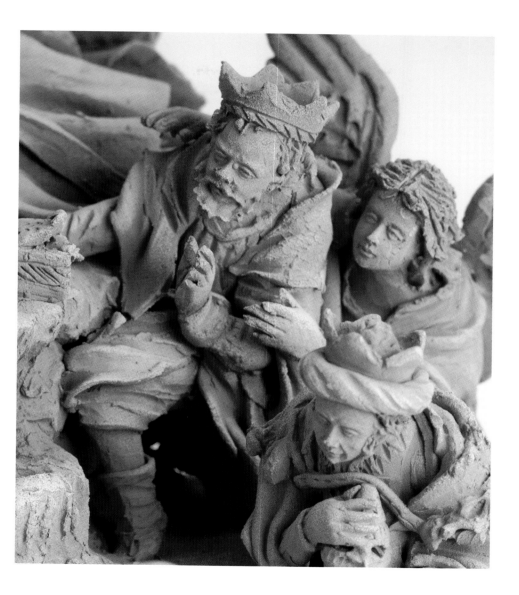

ITALY
+
FRANCESCO SCARLATELLA

TERRA-COTTA

Francesco Scarlatella is one of many clay artists living and working in Caltagirone, a Sicilian city, sometimes called the "city of crèches," that has been a ceramics center for centuries. Scarlatella, who was born in 1951, has worked with clay for nearly four decades and considers himself a self-taught artist, although he has received some help from his brother, Ignazio, who has had some formal art education.

Scarlatella's works are primarily unpainted terra-cotta, but he also occasionally incorporates wood or volcanic stone from the region of Mount Etna, and applies color to some pieces. He considers his style to be in the tradition of Giacomo Bongiovanni-Vaccaro (1772–1859), who lived in Caltagirone in the eighteenth century and is arguably Sicily's most famous sculptor.

Scarlatella has always sculpted religious works, but has devoted himself especially to making *presepi* (crèches) since

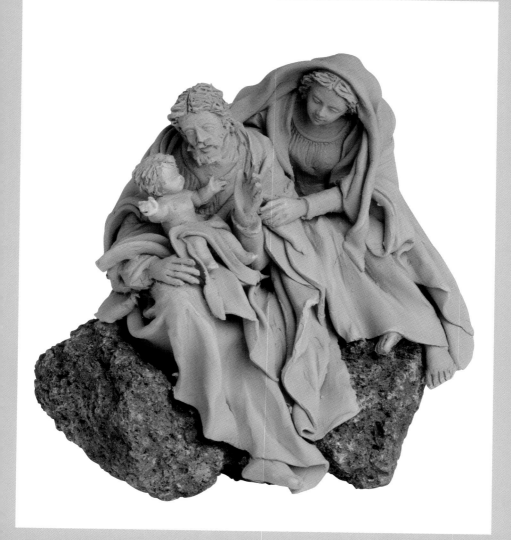

the mid-1980s. He finds "spiritual grace" in his scenes and often identifies himself with the shepherd figures. Two of his *presepi* are in the Vatican Museum's collections.

In the large crèche commissioned for the Govan collection (opposite), the kings arrive with their gifts. An angel guides one of them toward the Infant, and a shepherd welcomes another. One angel holds a book, perhaps the Old Testament. Joseph looks on, and Mary lies beside the Baby Jesus. The smaller crèche (previous page), also commissioned, is unusual, since Joseph is holding the Infant. Mary tenderly embraces Joseph as she looks on. The figures are placed on a lava stone from Mount Etna.

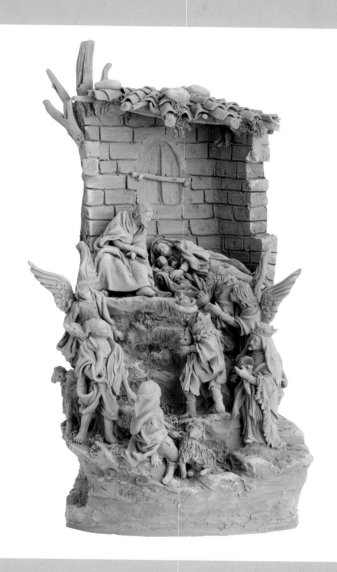

ARIZONA, USA

✦

THOMAS AND ELSIE FRANCO

SAGUARO CACTUS

This crèche, primarily made of cactus, was commissioned for the collection. It was made by Thomas Franco, a Wa:k Tohono O'odham, with the help of his wife, Elsie, who is Tohono O'odham. Thomas's parents, Domingo and Chepa Franco, were well-known carvers who also created crèches, and were among the first Native Americans to make nativities in the mid-twentieth century. Thomas's rustic-looking scenes are in a style similar to his parents'. In this crèche, all the figures are carved from the woody ribs that support the main stem of the saguaro cactus. The stable (a *ramada*, or shelter) is also made from saguaro. The loglike pieces of the roof come from the ends of the ribs. Elsie dressed the figures, giving them real hair and making their sandals, and applied the hides to the sheep and dog. Among the many unique features of this striking crèche is the placement of the Infant Jesus in a hammock.

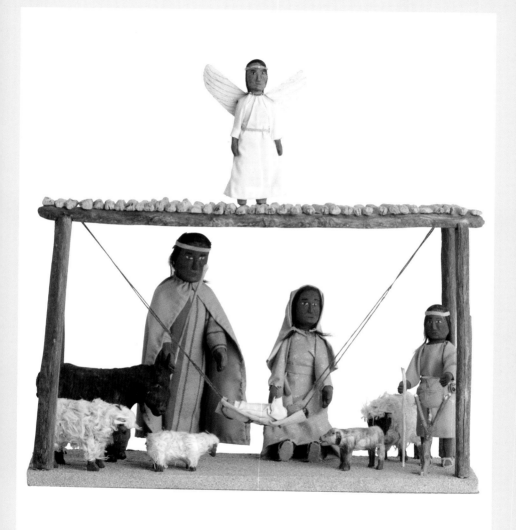

ARGENTINA
WICHI PEOPLE
CHAGUAR FIBER

This scene was made by Wichi women living in Los Blancos, Argentina. The Wichi people, numbering perhaps only 30,000 today, live in the northwestern part of the country, near the borders with Bolivia and Paraguay. Formerly semi-nomadic, they now live on marginal land, retaining their own language and much of their culture. They are one of the few Native American communities remaining in Argentina, and are mostly Christian.

In this depiction, the Holy Family is covered by a *toldo*, a canopy like those that Wichi women use today to shield themselves from the sun as they work. The spartan setting reflects the simple life led by this community, and the earthen colors reflect the native landscape. The distinctive cultural feel is heightened by the medium used. This "chaguar" crèche features fiber thread that derives from the *caraguatá*, or chaguar, an indigenous plant belonging to the bromeliad family. Making the thread is a long, painstaking process.

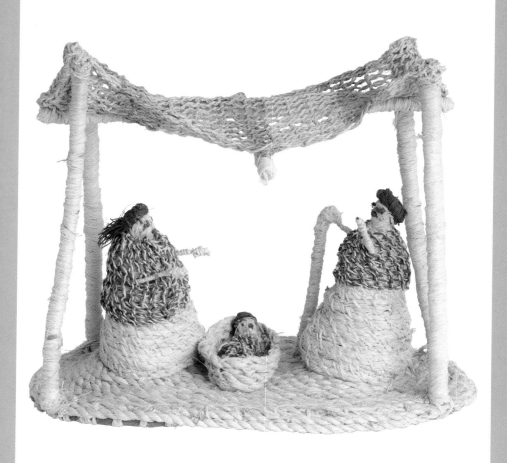

SINGAPORE
+
AMOS AND ALBERT TAY

CINNAMON PASTE

The Tay family enterprise of making incense sticks and figures from the wood of the cinnamon tree, ground to a paste, led to the idea of making nativities. Amos (born 1962) makes the figures and Albert (born 1959) the stables.

Figures of straw-covered wire are wrapped with sheets of cinnamon paste and sculpted. As Taoists, the Tays' interest in the Nativity is merely artistic, and they have created both Chinese and Western examples for about twenty years.

In this Chinese crèche, the lavishly adorned kings are drawn from characters in Chinese literature. Mary resembles the Taoist Goddess of Mercy, Kuan Yin, while the Christ Child is presented as a commoner. The striking angel figure

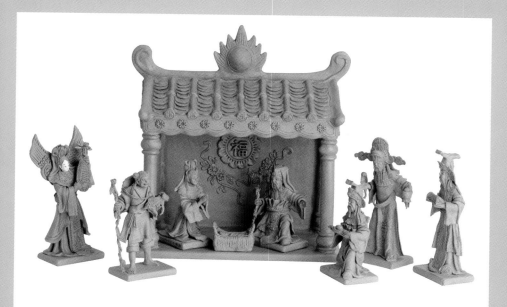

plays a traditional *pipa*, and its white mask is inspired by the painted white faces of Chinese opera.

In my search for a Singaporean crèche, I met the late sculptor Brother Joseph McNally and his assistant, Catherine Chua, who were visiting the United States. I asked for Catherine's help in obtaining a crèche from the Tays, about whom a friend had told me. She ordered the nativity, helped with shipment, and even generously paid for the angel as a gift.

IVORY COAST
UNKNOWN ARTIST
BRONZE

One of the most elegant crèches in the collection, this bronze Holy Family comes from Abidjan, the capital of Ivory Coast. This piece may have been made by artisans from Burkina Faso, who live in the city's Adjame district. Each figure is finely constructed, and the composition conveys tenderness and warmth. Mary gazes intently at the sleeping Child as if pondering the miraculous birth, and Joseph's tall, protective figure bows to Mary and the Infant, giving the entire piece a gentle, loving atmosphere.

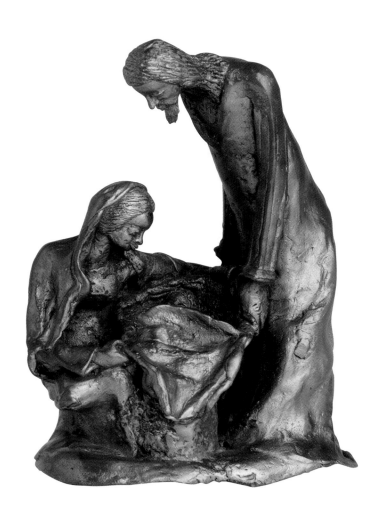

IRELAND

THE WILD GOOSE STUDIO

POWDERED METAL

This Irish crèche in bas-relief was made using powdered iron bonded with resin through a process called cold cast. It was created by the Wild Goose Studio of Kinsale, County Cork, a studio known for creating religious, Celtic, and secular objects. The Wild Goose Studio commissioned and purchased the design for the crèche from Nell Murphy, a distinguished Irish sculptor. The cold-cast process results in pieces with a thick outer shell of durable metal (in this case, iron), backed by a resin compound.

144

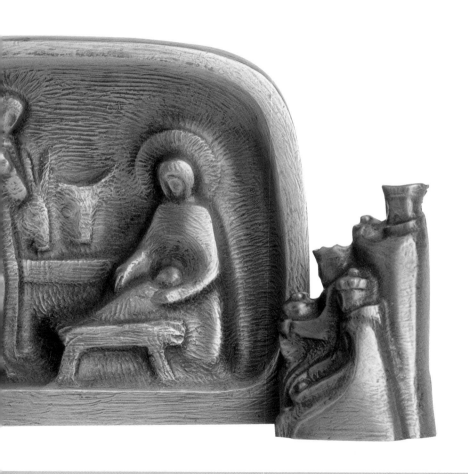

TAIWAN
+
UNKNOWN ARTIST
BAMBOO

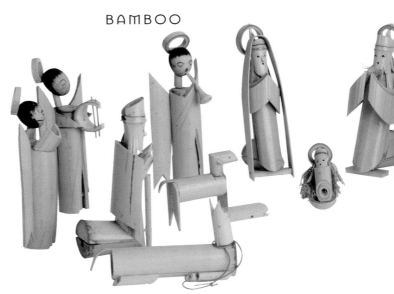

The origin of this delightful bamboo crèche is uncertain. It was given to me by a friend from my parish, St. Ann Catholic Church in Arlington, Virginia. She in turn had received it from a missionary priest who brought it from China around 1960, making it one of the older crèches in

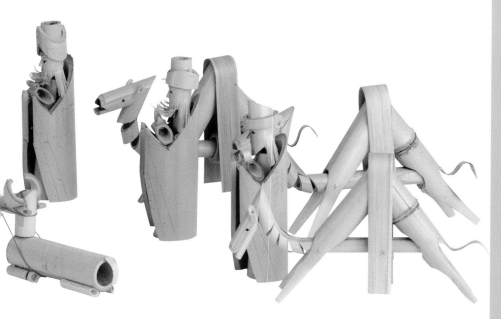

the collection. Bamboo crèches are made in the southern part of Taiwan, and it is likely that this one comes from that region. In this skillfully worked piece, Chinese red cords or ropes adorn the animals, and the camels are particularly fanciful. Angels play instruments as they greet the magi.

BELARUS

LUBOV SELIVONCHIK

STRAW

Straw is a medium used widely in Belarus to create utilitarian, decorative, and artistic objects. Through one of Belarus's leading authorities on straw art, Tatiana Repina, I contacted Lubov Selivonchik, whom Repina considers to be a "magnificent artist." Selivonchik (born 1958) lives in Minsk. Educated as an architect, she found limited opportunities in her professional field. In 1996, she began work with the Belarusian national crafts center and was encouraged to create with straw. Her drawing skills as an architect helped her especially to design and make straw objects that suggest moving forms.

Selivonchik likes making animals and dolls. Although she had made Madonna figures, she had never before created a nativity, and was touched by making this, her first. Repina informed me that Selivonchik, who considers herself a spiritual person, was inspired as she made it, and it is now one of her favorites. She looks forward to making more.

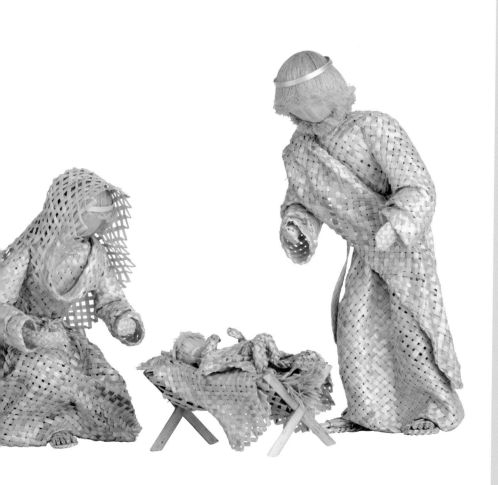

NIGERIA
UNKNOWN ARTIST

THORN WOOD

Thorn-wood carving is an art form that developed in the twentieth century in the southwestern region of Nigeria, and is unique to Africa. The thorns come from varieties of silk-cotton trees and have dark, light, or reddish shades. Since the size of the thorns is limited, ranging from 2 to 4 inches (5–10 cm), carvers glue many pieces together to form sometimes simple, sometimes expansive, scenes of the Nativity, as well as of everyday life.

This crèche was a gift for the collection from USAID friends. The finely carved figures reflect their African character, and the little angels climbing about the stable roof add a humorous, happy note.

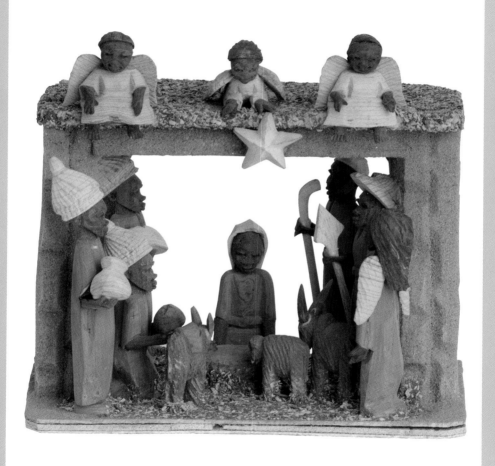

WEST BANK
✦
UNKNOWN ARTIST

OLIVE WOOD

Olive-wood carvings from the Holy Land are familiar throughout the Western world. The olive branch has long been a symbol of peace: in the book of Genesis, the end of the flood is signaled by an olive twig brought by a dove to Noah. Olive is a hardwood cherished for its beautiful tones and grain. Such carvings as this Holy Family scene, which comprises just one piece of wood, are made using branches taken during pruning.

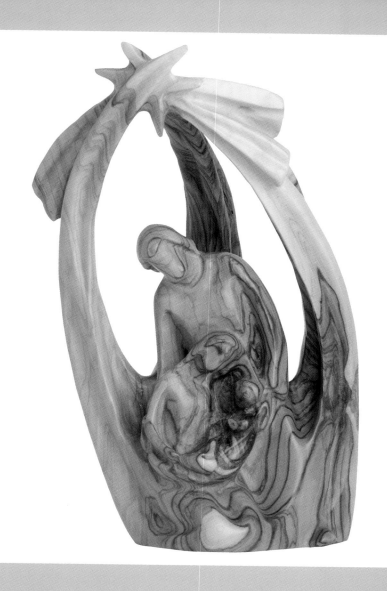

PERU
✦
NICARIO JIMÉNEZ QUISPE
POTATO CLAY

The *retablo* crèche is a shrinelike box popular in the Andes. Nicario Jiménez Quispe (see also pages 34–35) is among Peru's most celebrated folk artists, and has expanded the *retablo* art form by creating historical and political scenes. He began carving at age seven or eight, and learned to make *retablos* from his father. He creates single or layered scenes in a box, or even triptychs, often with scores of figures. He uses a small piece of sharpened wood to shape the figures, before air-drying, assembling, and painting

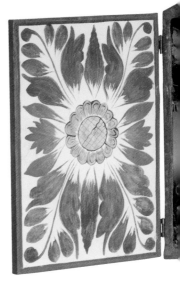

them. The figures in this crèche are made from a "clay" of potato and plaster of Paris. The scene reflects Jiménez's blending of Andean culture with Catholicism: a joyful fiesta celebrates the Nativity, which appears almost lost in the

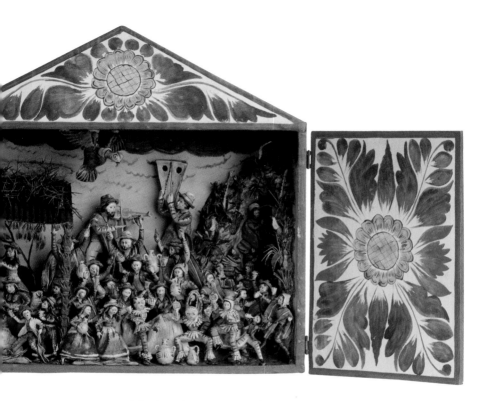

upper right-hand corner. At the top is a condor, a symbol of power among native Peruvians, and, for Jiménez, a messenger from God. On the left, villagers make *checha*, a local drink of fermented corn.

SEASON OF GIVING

✦

ACTS OF GENEROSITY

Christians believe that the Christ Child came to give his life for us, so that we might live. In turn, the wise men brought gifts for him. In many ways, the crèche tradition embodies this spirit of giving. Our family began collecting crèches more than thirty years ago, and over the decades the help of friends and the kindness of strangers have enhanced our journey of collecting. The generous contributions of friends—both old and newly met along the way—have made the journey a gift in itself.

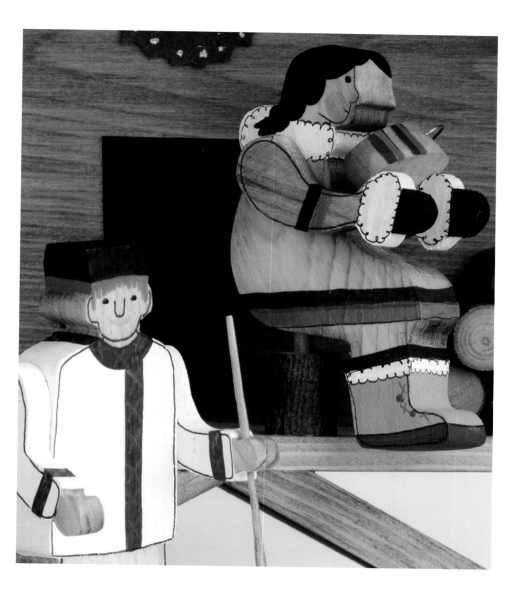

RUSSIA
✢
LILIA SHEVCHENKO

Three-dimensional crèches are a Western tradition uncommon in Orthodox Russia. My search—not an easy one—for a Russian example led me to a website for the Most Holy Mother of God Catholic Church, Vladivostok, and I was delighted to learn that the pastor was an American, Father Myron Effing. He kindly agreed to inquire on our behalf, but I heard no more, and was greatly surprised when he contacted me from California almost two years later, bringing a crèche in his suitcase! Apparently a member of his parish, Lilia Shevchenko, made children's puppets and had readily agreed to make a crèche. I was humbled to learn that she sought no compensation; however, I made a contribution to the church.

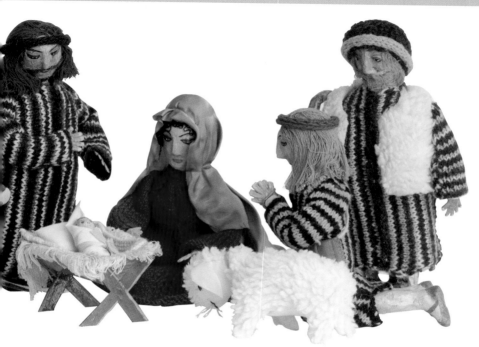

The papier-mâché figures are clothed in knitted garments, and the shepherd's vest is of lamb's wool. The animals are made from carefully chosen fabrics. In receiving this crèche, we were touched both that Shevchenko generously offered her work to strangers abroad, and that Father Effing had remembered my request over such a long period of time.

THE PHILIPPINES
THE CARLOS FAMILY

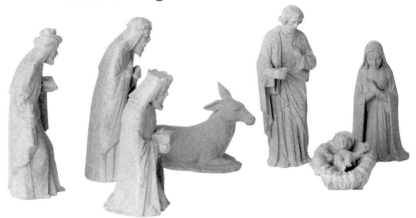

This crèche was a generous gift from Salvador and Gigi Carlos of Manila, leading crèche collectors in the Philippines, whom we first contacted simply to inquire about the development of the nativity tradition in the Philippines. Over the course of several years, they kindly gave us three crèches, including this one, which was created by the family.

Crèches in the Philippines are made from many materials. This one is made in one of the more unusual media in the collection: "ash ware" (volcanic ash and resin). The late

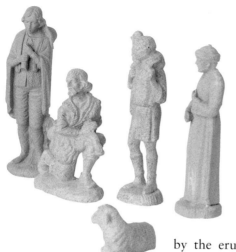

Salvador Lichauco-Carlos began experimenting with the ash deposited on his roof by the eruption of Mount Pinatubo in 1991 by mixing it with resin and pouring the blend into molds. One of the first objects he made in this way was a crucifix that was presented to the country's then president, Corazón Aquino. Salvador trained one of his former employees to make this crèche set, using molds of Italian or Spanish origin for the figures. Several of the figures here resemble those in our first crèche, an Italian piece that Emilia and I acquired in 1962 (see page 14).

jAPAN
+
MitSUKi KUMEKAWA

Finding an artist-made crèche from Japan proved very difficult. Luckily, I made contact with the American ceramist Tom Morris of the Agape Ceramic Studio (now in Yokohama). Tom asked one of his former students to make a crèche for me. Mitsuki Kumekawa (born 1932), a distinguished professor emeritus of Japanese literature and culture, now writes, paints, and makes ceramics. He taught in the United States at Princeton University and at universities in Singapore as well as in his native Japan. This crèche, made of *gotomaki* clay with a *shino* glaze, combines Western, Christian form with a Japanese ceramic technique paying homage to longstanding Asian influences. Kumekawa's glazing and firing technique—including "reduction-firing" in a charcoal kiln—gave the figures antique-looking cracks. Tom says this traditional Japanese style "creates a rough, textured and earthy look compared

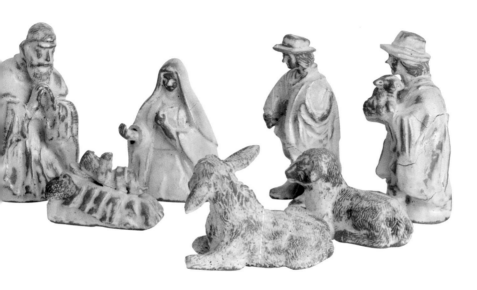

to the smooth, clean, bright colors associated with many European ceramic wares."

The touching aspect of this scene is that its creator is steeped in the traditions of his own culture but open to other forms of religious expression. Kumekawa had never made a crèche. There was no reason for him to accept my request, but he did so with dedication. He wrote, "Though I am not a Christian, I feel very much honor."

ANGOLA
CARLOS JOÃO ANTONIO

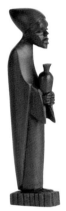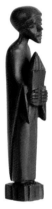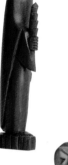

Crafts were sparse in Angola, which had endured a civil war. Nevertheless, I was fortunate to commission this crèche through a USAID colleague and his friend Father Agustin Escelera, who found the carver, yet another example of Africa's unheralded talent. Both Father Escelera and Carlos João Antonio offered the crèche to me as a gift, in a humbling gesture of charity from people with few material resources. In return I sent Father Escelera a box of school supplies.

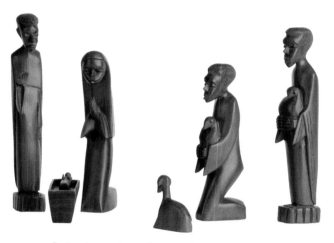

João Antonio, a farmer, began carving in the early 1990s in his mid-thirties, and his work includes other religious art. The pieces in this scene, beautifully crafted from Angolan blackwood, conform to a traditional format while reflecting indigenous characteristics. The kings bear gifts in elaborate vessels, and their caps recall those of the wise men from Phrygia who appear in some of the earliest depictions of the Nativity in the catacombs of Rome. Although Mary is simply sculpted, her youthful face expresses deep devotion.

UGANDA
✦
NYANGI-BOSCO

While the collection consists largely of three-dimensional crèches, it does include a few attractive plaques or relief carvings, such as this handsome example, a gift from a USAID friend. The artist, Nyangi-Bosco, is developing a reputation for his fine carving. Working just outside Kampala, this relatively young man has begun to employ others, whom he teaches. The scene is a rural village setting with a thatch-roofed hut, tropical trees, and people in native dress. The three kings carry their gifts in baskets. The wood is mavulu, an African hardwood often used in carving.

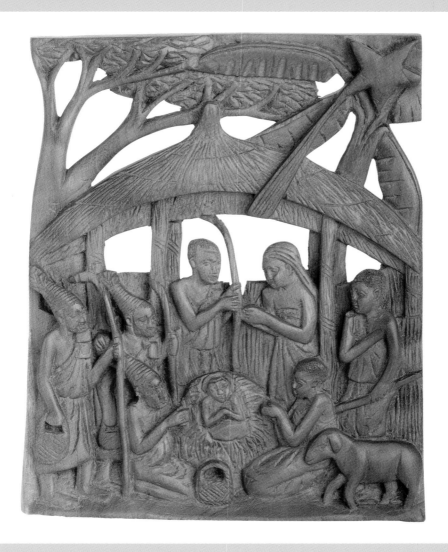

ARIZONA, USA
+ FELIX YAZZIE

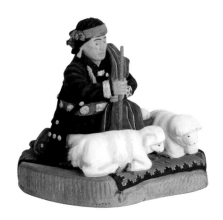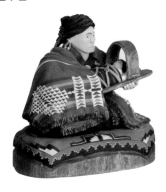

Through the help of a kind priest we were able to acquire a Navajo crèche—a considerable feat, since Navajo artists rarely make crèches, being better known for weaving and pottery. Navajo Christian imagery is limited, since only a small proportion of the people have adopted the faith; also, Navajo religion and culture do not encourage figural representation.

Eventually, I read about a Catholic priest, Father Blane Grein, in Chinle, Arizona, who worked with the Navajo

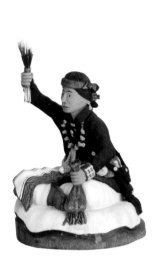

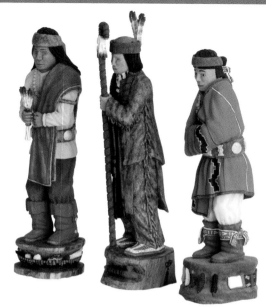

people. I contacted him to ask if he knew anyone who might make a crèche, and luckily a local artist, Felix Yazzie, had recently created a carving for the church. Happily, Yazzie agreed to Father Grein's request to make a crèche for me, and the result is one of the finest artworks in our collection. The Holy Family is in the style of the *Dine* ("people"), as the Navajo call themselves; Mary and Joseph wear typical attire, and their hair is styled in Navajo buns. The kings represent the Apache and Ute people.

169

MONTANA, USA
+
HANNEKE AND LES IPPISCH

I had always wanted an Alaskan nativity, and eventually bought one online from a shop in Juneau. My disappointment on learning that its creators actually lived in Montana turned to humility and awe after I contacted them and discovered Hanneke Ippisch's heroic story, one of the best examples of how the collection is enriched beyond the cultures and art it represents.

Hanneke (born 1925), the daughter of a Protestant minister, was born in The Netherlands and joined the wartime resistance movement. In January 1945, she was captured and held in a small cell for weeks, in cold, darkness, and hunger, before the end of hostilities brought her release.

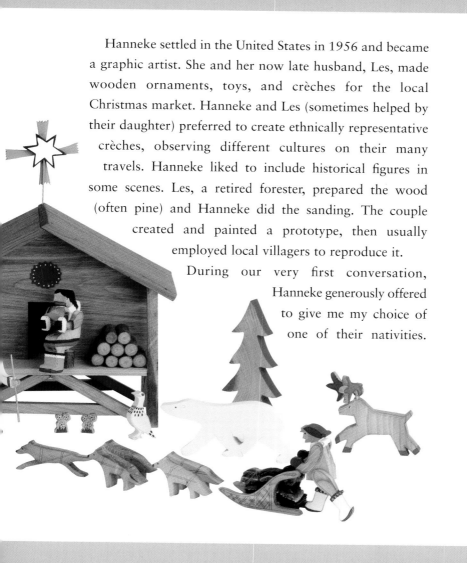

Hanneke settled in the United States in 1956 and became a graphic artist. She and her now late husband, Les, made wooden ornaments, toys, and crèches for the local Christmas market. Hanneke and Les (sometimes helped by their daughter) preferred to create ethnically representative crèches, observing different cultures on their many travels. Hanneke liked to include historical figures in some scenes. Les, a retired forester, prepared the wood (often pine) and Hanneke did the sanding. The couple created and painted a prototype, then usually employed local villagers to reproduce it.

During our very first conversation, Hanneke generously offered to give me my choice of one of their nativities.

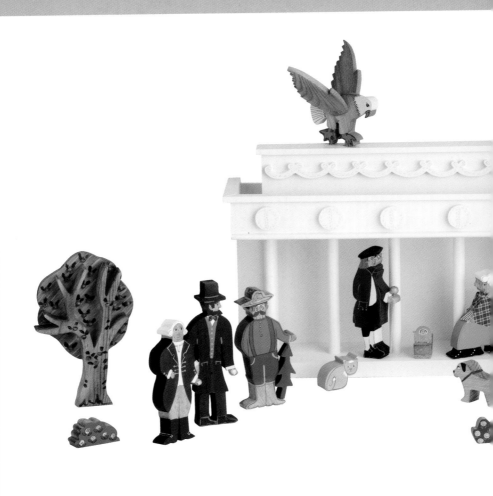

I could not resist the Washington-themed crèche (this page), since I live in the capital area: the "stable" is the Lincoln Memorial; Betsy Ross and Ben Franklin with the Infant represent the Holy Family; and the three kings are George Washington, Abraham Lincoln, and Teddy Roosevelt. Paul Revere arrives on horseback with his lantern, and the donkey and elephant symbolize the Democratic and Republican parties.

In the Alaska scene (previous pages), the stable is a cache, a storage structure on poles. Mary is in Eskimo dress; Joseph in Cossack dress. The three kings are a kayaker, a dog-sled driver, and a fisherman. However attractive and amusing— "just folk art," in Hanneke's words—these crèches become powerful when one realizes that they were created by someone (helped by a spouse) who has witnessed the depths to which humanity can sink.

MALAWI
✦
SUWEDI BIGULA

This scene by Suwedi Bigula reflects in so many ways the hope, love, and unity the crèche came to represent to Emilia and me (see also pages 124–25). Exquisitely carved, it represents the indigenous people of Malawi, yet speaks to all peoples. The scene transcends particular religious beliefs, in that the baby in the manger can be understood as the Incarnation by Christians, or, by others, in terms of the birth of a child that unites all humanity. The crèche's universality is exemplified by the fact that it was carved by a Muslim artisan under the auspices of a Catholic art center, and was found and given to us by a Jewish friend.

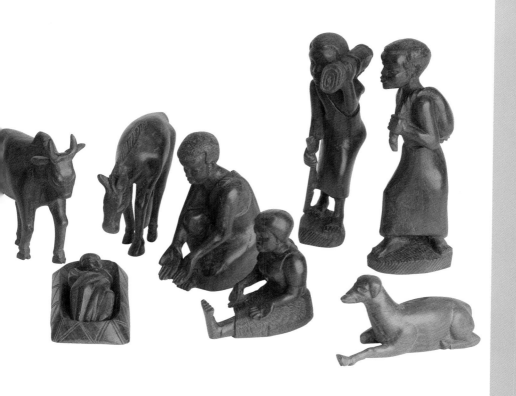

CROATiA
✦
STAПKO BUПIĆ

This striking crèche was commissioned with the help of Josip Barlek, senior curator of Zagreb's Ethnographic Museum. Stanko Bunić (born 1936), a self-taught folk artist, is one of the last Croatians to work in the naïve tradition in the northwestern region of the country. Bunić's interest in crèches stems from an illness and slow recovery: "[I] decided to model a crèche . . . . Crèches bring God closer to me; I give them to other people [to] wish them peace and prosperity." Poor health now limits his ability to make crèches, and he regrets that there is no one to continue the tradition.

These Croatian naïve scenes, like Krakovian *szopki* (see pages 36–37), are dominated by distinctive architectural settings. This setting is wooden, decorated with colored paper. In times past, the figures were also painted paper, ceramic, or wood, rather than the manufactured plastic pieces seen here. It is indeed sad that there are so few artisans left who make these delightful scenes.

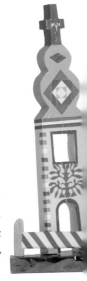

176

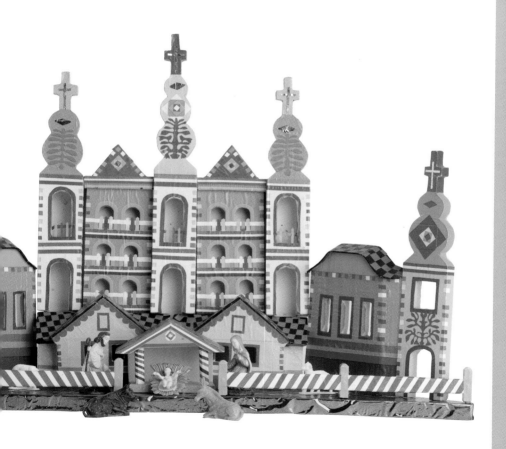

ALL IN THE FAMILY

✦

FAMILY LEGACIES

A crèche is a treasured possession and heirloom in many families. Our collection, however, includes many examples in which the crèche-making tradition itself, together with its legacy of faith, has been shared within families and between generations.

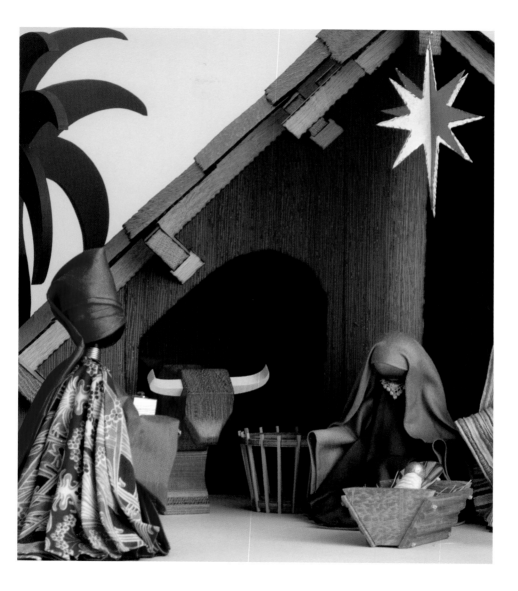

POLAND
+
WACLAW SUSKA

I first saw Waclaw Suska's work on the cover of Hans-Joachim Schauss's *Contemporary Polish Folk Artists* (1987). Emilia and I traveled to Poland with a list of carvers from the book, hoping to find a crèche. In Warsaw we bought one by Waclaw's son Stanislaw (see pages 182–83), and the shop's staff helped us find one by Waclaw. Years later, we also bought one by his son-in-law, Adam Wydra (see pages 184–85).

At twenty, Waclaw was sent to a German forced-labor factory, returning three years later, in 1945, to work as a carpenter building houses. In 1971, aged nearly fifty, and without formal training, Waclaw began carving "to . . . make myself feel better." Before his death in 1999, he won prizes and sold carvings in Europe and the United States.

This warmly colored crèche embodies a primitive realism. The faces are somber, perhaps from respect or devotion. Jesus's arms are extended, symbolizing his reaching out to humanity.

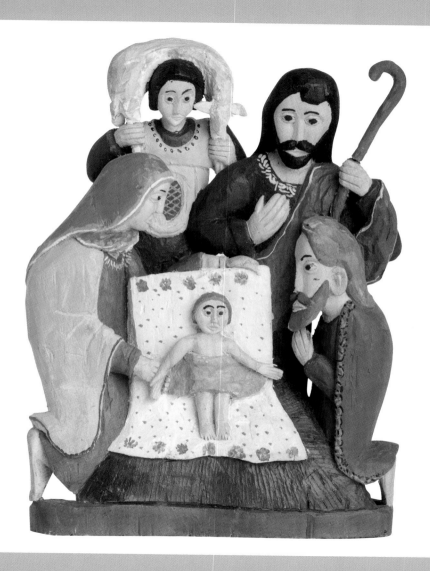

POLAND
+
STANISLAW SUSKA

S tanislaw Suska (born 1959) trained as a stonemason, and enjoyed and was encouraged by his father's sculpting. "My father was my teacher," he says. At age fourteen, Stanislaw created his first sculpture, a carving of a sorrowful Christ. Having now carved for more than a quarter of a century, Stanislaw sees it as "his mission and lifelong passion." Sacred themes—especially biblical stories—dominate his work. He carves single figures (particularly angels), historical figures, and bas-reliefs.

Stanislaw's lively carvings are sometimes in triptych form, and his scenes are crowded with many figures. In this compact presentation, the figures' facial expressions exude energy. This crèche conveys the excitement at the birth of Christ, who appears a little older than in many crèches, with the gesture of a young boy tugging at his mother's garment. The Christ Child often appears larger in scale than other figures in order to reflect his central importance.

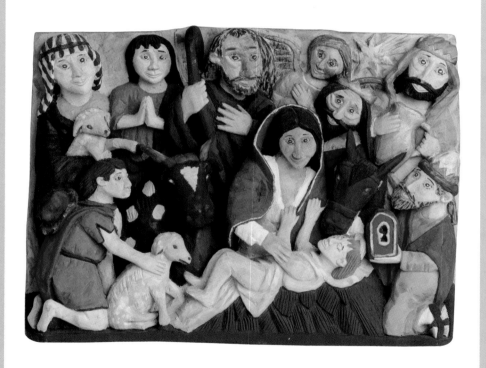

POLAND
✦
ADAM WYDRA

Born in 1953 in Lukow, Adam Wydra married Jadwiga, the daughter of distinguished artist Waclaw Suska (see pages 180–81). After a time, the couple moved to Waclaw's farm, where Wydra observed and learned from his father-in-law's carving. Wydra began to carve when he was twenty years old. His first piece was sold a year later, and in a short time he developed his own style.

Wydra carves both religious and secular-themed relief sculptures, triptychs, and single figures, using only three carving implements and no machinery. He also creates large outdoor sculptures that can reach 10 feet (3 m) high. His work has earned many awards and is exhibited widely.

Wydra carved crèches from the beginning of his career and says the Nativity is his favorite subject, giving him the most pleasure and satisfaction. In this scene, Wydra's figures are similar to Waclaw's but appear softer or, in his own words, "more gentle."

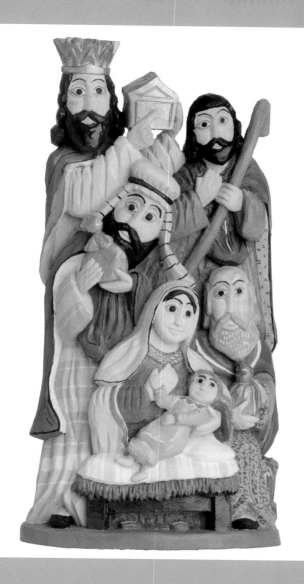

COSTA RICA
+ GOVAN

The name GOVAN gives this crèche a special place in the Govan Collection, although it is not a surname but the name of an enterprise formed by a couple, Juan José Gómez and Alexandra Vanolli de Gómez. Juan José, a dentist and university teacher, enjoys painting and sculpting, particularly making miniatures. He created a miniature nativity in a sphere for his wife for their first Christmas together, and this was the seed for their enterprise.

At first, Juan José created Costa Rican scenes without people or animals; later, he began to include figures. He enjoys creating images of daily life, such as women washing clothes, and scenes with environmental themes, such as endangered turtles. Holding "strong religious beliefs," he sees nativities as special among his works. His early portrayals consisted only of papier-mâché miniatures of the Holy Family; now he works with clay and adds other figures, as in this appealing landscape, which includes kings and sheep.

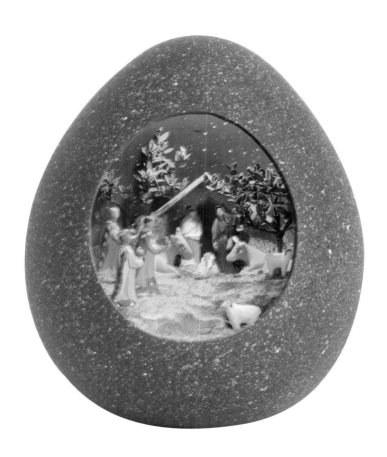

NORWAY
✦
THE ENGELSEN FAMILY

Henning Engelsen is one of Norway's leading carvers. He started a workshop, Henning Woodcarvers, in Toten in 1947, hoping "to create a world of figures that radiate joy and humanity." He carved such subjects as Vikings, fishermen, trolls, and—his favorite—horses. Now that he is retired, his work is continued by his daughters, Christl and Angelina, and Angelina's husband, Bjorne Espedal (as well as a few non-family employees).

The family wanted to create a Norwegian crèche with "distinctive medieval features." In 2000, Angelina and Christl designed and began to construct this elegant piece. Angelina and Bjorne carved; Christl determined the colors; and the other artisans assisted in the carving and finishing

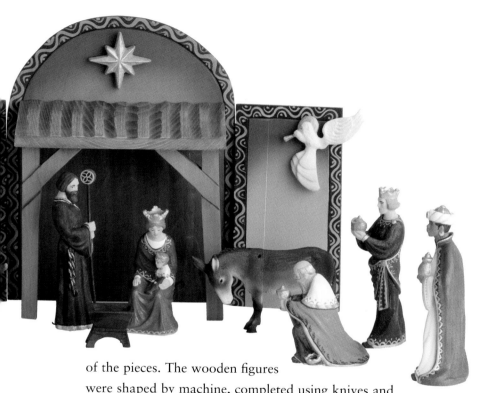

of the pieces. The wooden figures
were shaped by machine, completed using knives and
air tools, and hand-painted. Wearing a crown, Mary holds
the Infant on her lap. The depiction of the Virgin as a queen
is rare in a crèche.

UNITED KINGDOM
✦
JOAN AND DAVID KOTTLER

This appealing scene is the result of Joan and David Kottler's search for a nativity that would convey "the true mystery and wonder of Christmas" to their children. Disappointed with crèches they had seen in shops, Joan decided to create her own. In 1976, she began making crèches to sell to help the family earn money. In a few years,

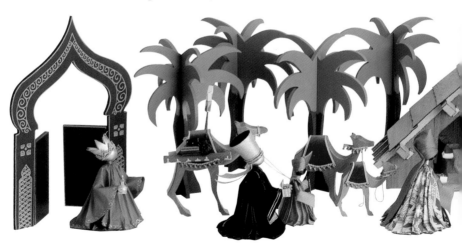

she developed the style seen here. Some figures have been added and others have evolved, but the scene has essentially remained the same.

Making these crèches is very much a family industry. At one time, two of the Kottlers' sons assisted with the effort, and, briefly, a few other workers were hired to help make the stables. Joan, trained as a teacher, does most of the work; David, a civil engineer, makes the animals. Neither is trained in woodwork. Machinery is used in the making of some of the wooden pieces, but not for the figures. David says the endeavor "has become a way of life for us."

This scene, with its Moorish arch, includes both exotic and humble elements of the Nativity story. The kings' rich costumes contrast with those of the shepherds and Holy Family. All the clothing is made of stiffened fabric, and the animals of polished hardwood. The stable, made by both Joan and David, is of oak and oak veneer.

MEXICO
✦
IRENE AGUILAR

As a young girl, Irene Aguilar attended less than a year of school before she was needed at home to care for one of her brothers. She remembers playing with clay as a small child, and sculpting figures when she was eight. By the end of her teenage years, she was creating group scenes to make money to pay for medicine for her mother. She has since received national recognition for her work. Irene's piece in the collection might be described as a nativity fruit bowl. The traditional figures, facing outward, are placed around the rim of the bowl. Irene's palette—like that of her sisters—comprises varied and vivid colors.

Irene and her three sisters (see pages 194–99) are among the most famous ceramists in Mexico today. Most of my information about them derives from the book *Oaxacan Ceramics* (2000) by Lois Wasserspring.

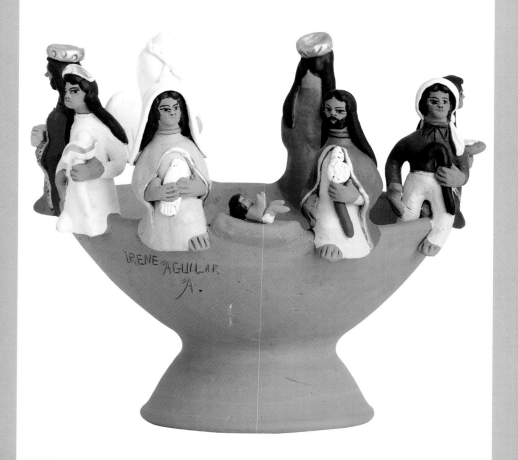

MEXICO
✦
JOSEFINA AGUILAR

Josefina, the second oldest of the four Aguilar sisters—probably the most famous ceramists in Mexico today—was the first to gain fame for her ceramics, and is probably the best known. Working on her own while still very young, she first received recognition for her ceramics in her early twenties. In just a few years, she attracted attention in both Europe and the United States, and she continues to be one of the most prominent folk artists in Mexico. Josefina's crèche is vividly colored. Her figures tend to reflect the features of the local

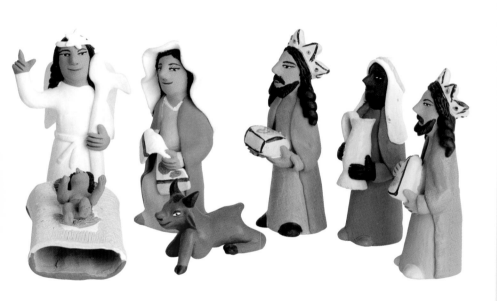

people, the Zapotecs. Joseph clutches a large flowering plant that appears to be his staff. Other elements, such as the star that rests on the angel's head at the center of the composition, add a touch of whimsy.

MEXICO
✦
GUILLERMINA AGUILAR

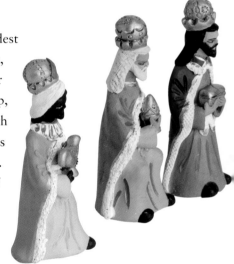

Guillermina Aguilar is the eldest of the four Aguilar sisters, but she began her career after her sister Josefina. While growing up, Guillermina worked with clay with her mother (whose own work was for years signed by her husband). In 1968, almost as an act of desperation to provide for her growing family, Guillermina turned to ceramics. Ten years later, she began to gain recognition. She has exhibited internationally and, according to Lois Wasserspring's book *Oaxacan Ceramics*, "has even, on occasion, acted as Mexico's 'folk art ambassador abroad.'" Guillermina's crèche features the vibrant colors seen in so much of the sisters' work. The

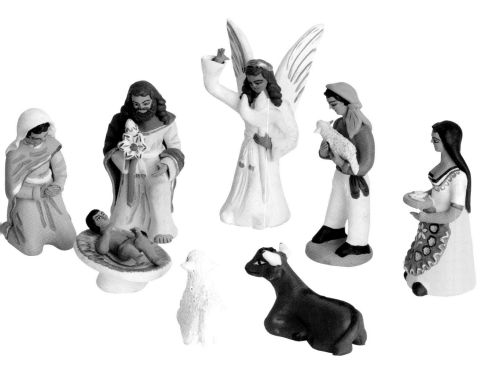

kings have contrasting beards, and the angel, with a staff, is similar to the one depicted in Concepción's crèche (see pages 198–99). Joseph holds a lily, and the Christ Child reaches out.

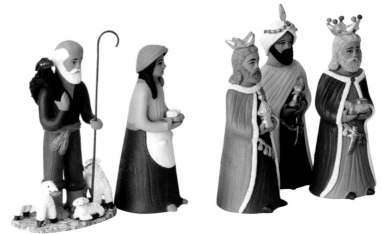

Despite the Aguilar sisters' successes, Lois Wasserspring notes in her book *Oaxacan Ceramics* that life has not been easy, especially for Concepción, the youngest of the four. Concepción was only ten when her mother died, after which she spent much of her time caring for her younger brothers. She did not turn to ceramics until 1978 and not in a dedicated way until 1988. Two years later, she gained recognition with a national award. Concepción's colors are

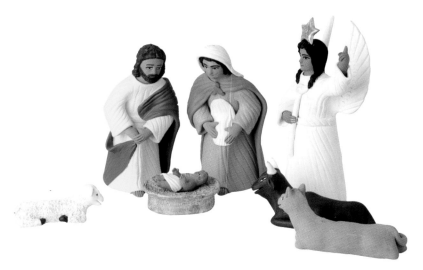

strong and exuberant, like those used by her sisters. The commanding angel, crowned with a star, points heavenward while announcing the birth of Jesus. The kings are resplendent in their bright robes and jeweled crowns, while the shepherdess looks on with a serene expression that exudes piety. The shepherd injects a touch of humor and earthiness, holding a black sheep across his shoulder while a white sheep happily chomps on grass.

COLOMBIA
+
PAULA CUELLAR

This colorful crèche was created by artist Paula Cuellar of Personitas de Colección, a family enterprise in Bogotá. Cuellar's artistic career began with her making dolls. People's reactions to her work encouraged her to initiate a family business in her grandmother's house. Much of the work is undertaken by the family, including Cuellar's mother, who is also an artist. Other women artisans are hired when needed. The figures are richly clothed in suede and leather, a characteristic of Cuellar's creations. The ceramic faces and hands are hand-painted.

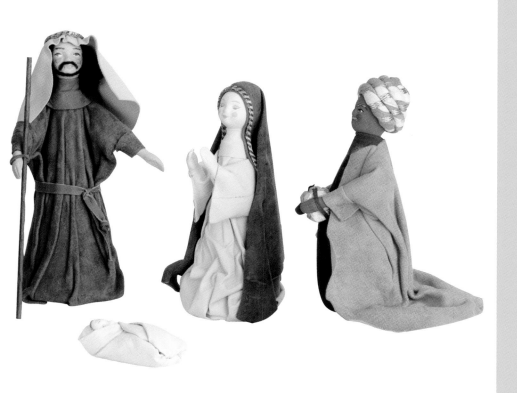

PERU
THE MAMANI FAMILY

Cristóbal Mamani, who has worked in ceramics for nearly forty years, learned his craft from his grandparents. He passed it on to Melchora, his wife, and their seven children. Today they work together in Lima, although the family's roots are in the Cuzco area of the Andes. They typically make religious sculptures, but also create pieces illustrating Andean life. They like to reflect Peru's various cultures, and this crèche represents the Shipibo, a tribe of perhaps 35,000 living in the Amazonian jungle. Most Shipibo are Christian, but they retain their strong preconversion cultural identity and way of life. In this clay scene, the clothes are decorated with a Shipibo design. The people bring gifts from the jungle: vegetables, fruit, a turtle, and a monkey. A tapir and a wild pig join the gathering. Jesus's exaggerated size is an example of the custom that uses proportion to signify relative importance.

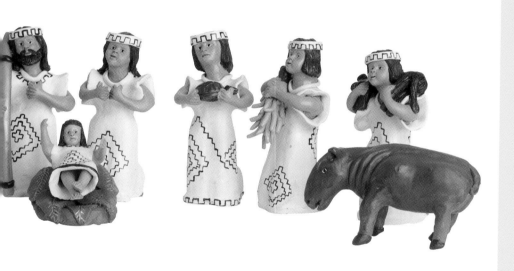

MAINE, USA
RUTH TEWKSBURY AND FAMILY

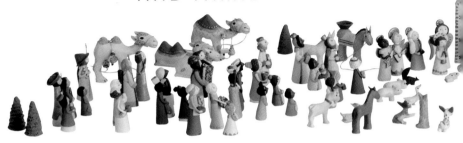

Emilia and I discovered the Tewksbury crèche in a shop in Kennebunkport during a vacation to Maine in 1979, and have acquired new pieces every year. Ruth Tewksbury conceived this scene in the 1970s and continually added new figures; it is still being expanded by her family.

Ruth, a medical technologist, needed a channel for her artistic interests. She began working with clay, and was inspired to create a crèche after seeing a picture of an ornately painted Mexican one. For years, Ruth made the people and her daughter Deborah Dunham the animals. By 1988, another daughter, Marie Cole, had begun

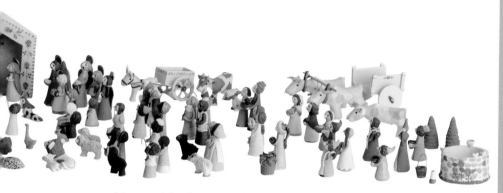

working with her, as had Marie's daughter, Dawn Wheatley, who assumed Deborah's role. Dawn's husband, Dan, joined the family enterprise in 1998. One of Ruth's last innovations before her death in 1991 was to introduce black figures for characters other than the black king. Dawn later introduced Asian figures. Both Marie and Dawn felt "a strong need to continue Ruth's legacy."

Each individually made parian-clay piece is hand-painted with underglazes before being fired. Gold enamel, when used, is applied after firing. All creation seems to be present; there is even a unicorn.

SPAIN

✦

BELENES PUIG S.L.

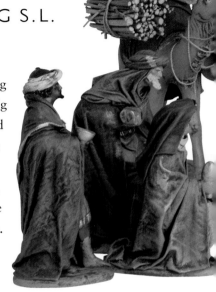

The Puig family's nativity-making began in 1933, when José Puig started to make cork stables and other elements of crèche scenes; in 1945, he began making terra-cotta figures. His son and daughter-in-law, Francisco and Mercedes, now run the family business with their sons. "Born among nativity figures," they are committed to continuing the family tradition, and oversee the design of the classical figures, even the way the fabric is glued to the figures and which colors are used.

The Puigs have made this form of crèche, with variations, for more than twenty years. They consider this version one of their "classics." It was influenced by the style of Francisco Salzillo, a renowned eighteenth-century sculptor

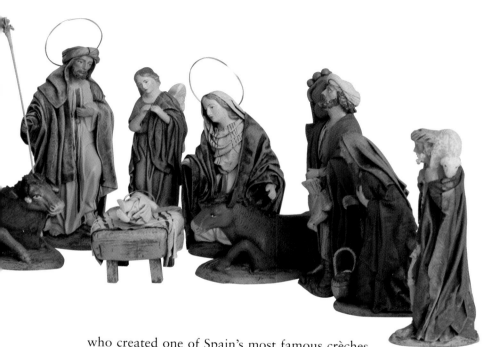

who created one of Spain's most famous crèches,
which consists of more than 500 pieces and reflects
the Baroque style of Salzillo's Italian father, Nicola. The
Puig figures are made of terra-cotta using molds, sun-dried,
and then hand-painted. Clothes made from stiffened fabrics
lavishly adorn each figure.

MAKING A DIFFERENCE

✦

CRÈCHES AS INSTRUMENTS OF SOCIAL CHANGE

The demand for crèches has created opportunities for skills training and employment where they might not otherwise exist. Supported by Catholic and Protestant missionaries, local government programs, and private individuals, these opportunities often arise in places and among peoples not normally associated with the crèche tradition.

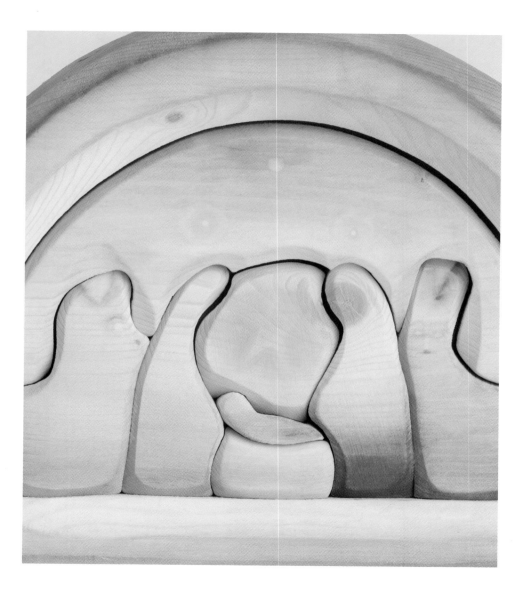

BOLIVIA
+
ARTESANIA SORATA

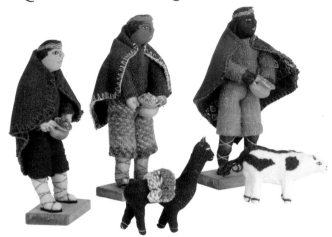

Artesania Sorata (founded in 1978 by Diane Bellomy), consists mostly of women. It aims to revive traditional textile arts while improving the native people's income and standard of living. Its dolls have been used in crèches for some years. Bellomy suggested the traditional "Inca dance" costume for the kings; the rest of the design represents the clothes worn by the Aymara people. This crèche was made by artisans from either the Adelio Quispe or Pastor Mendoza

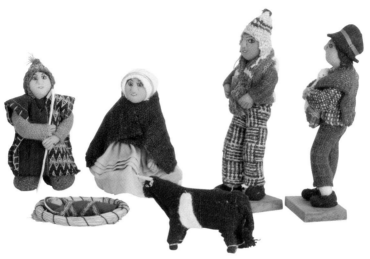

family, in Pocobaya in northern Bolivia. The kings' capes are made of traditional cloths (perhaps thirty to forty years old) called *aguayos*, which the local women use for many purposes, including carrying infants. The fabrics are hand-spun and hand-woven on traditional indigenous looms; factory-made cotton muslin is also used. One shepherd holds a panpipe, another a sheep. The kings bring the traditional gifts of gold and real frankincense and myrrh.

INDONESIA

SUKODONO MENNONITE WOOD-CARVERS

The wood-carvers of Sukodono, Indonesia, receive support from the Mennonite Central Committee (MCC) to enable them to earn income. The purpose of the carvers' group is to help provide employment, but also to sustain cultural traditions. Taman Petra is a cofounder of the Sukodono carvers. As a fourth-generation carver, Petra represents the strong cultural attachment to carving that exists in the Japara region. A master carver, he trains young apprentices on the front porch of his home. This crèche reflects the culture of the

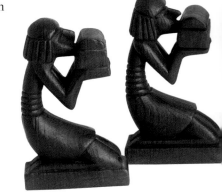

Asmats, who, numbering fewer than 100,000, live in the province of Irian Jaya. The Asmats were largely unknown to the rest of the world until the mid-twentieth century.

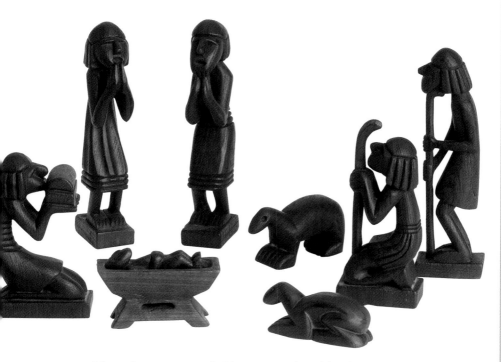

Many have accepted Christianity but blend it with their ancestor worship and animist beliefs. This stylized crèche conveys both reverence and the tribal character of the Asmat people.

213

CAMEROON
+
ARTISANS OF PRESCRAFT

This crèche was made by artisan Emmanuel Che, working with the Presbyterian Handicraft Center (Prescraft), which was founded by a Swiss missionary but is now managed locally in Cameroon. Nearly 600 artisans, mostly women, practice crafts—including making crèches—in three rural production centers. These brass pieces are produced by a method known as the lost-wax process. While the figures are made from a mold, at Prescraft the mold is destroyed each time. Each piece is therefore unique.

Emmanuel Che, trained by Prescraft, has worked for the organization as well as for himself since 1978, and lives in Bamenda. He produces a variety of articles in brass, including candleholders, animals, and decorative items, and he sometimes also works with copper.

In this Holy Family scene, Mary, simply clad, sits on a stool, and Joseph is represented deep in prayer.

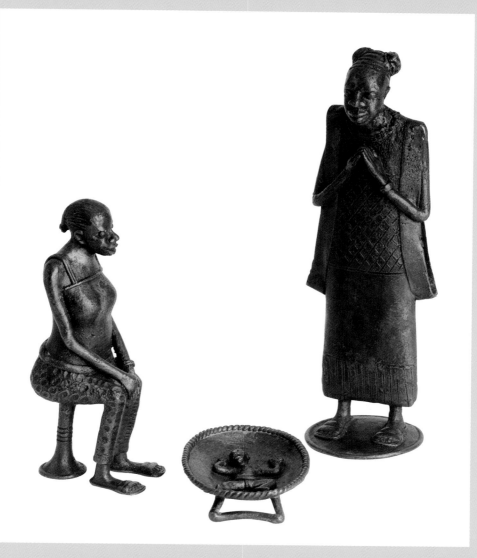

WEST BANK
✦
YWCA

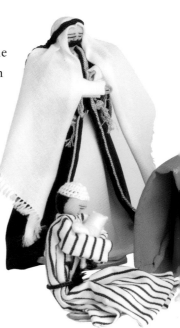

Women artisans supported by the Young Women's Christian Association (YWCA) of Jerusalem created this colorful scene. It was made by a group of about twenty young Palestinian women in the Jalazone Refugee Camp. The women also produce dolls dressed in national costumes. The Holy Family and the shepherds are dressed in traditional Palestinian clothes: Mary and Joseph are especially attractively adorned. This crèche was a gift from a Jewish friend who was a colleague at USAID.

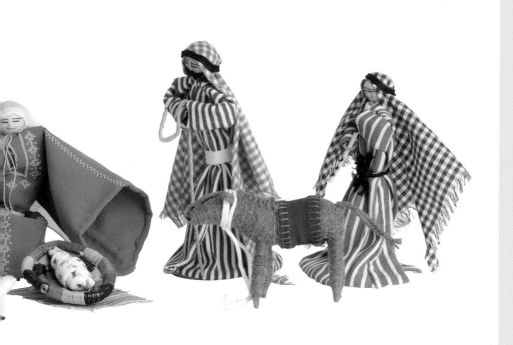

ΠEPAL
✦
ASSOCIATIOΠ OF
CRAFT PRODUCERS

The nonprofit Association for Craft Producers has existed in Kathmandu since 1984 to help train low-income artisans and provide a marketing outlet. The association works with about one thousand artisans, mostly women. The organization obtained guidance for a crèche design from outside buyers and created a prototype in its workshop; the women then produced the crèches in their homes.

The most striking feature is the stable, which resembles a traditional Nepalese house. It includes a sculptural centerpiece of a peacock. Peacocks are often included in Nepalese carvings and other designs: the feathers, used in

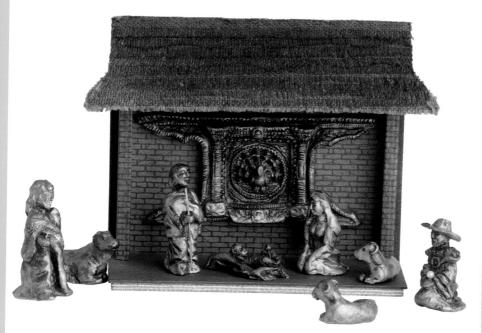

religious ceremonies, are considered auspicious and protective. The figures are made of clay. Two kings bear gifts modeled in gold; the third brings a pearl. The Baby Jesus lies in the manger with arms outstretched, as in many classic Italian presentations. Like several others, this crèche was a gift from USAID friends.

CAMBODIA
✦
BANTEAY PRIEB PRODUCTION

Banteay Prieb Production, or the Center of the Dove, is part of a Jesuit-supported program in Cambodia, and provides training for disabled people, including landmine victims. I learned about it from a Maryknoll missionary in Phnom Penh, Father Charles Dittmeier, who put me in touch with Jesuit Brother In Young Cho, a Korean affiliated with the workshop. The Center had previously made two or three nativities with only the Holy Family; this crèche—made for the collection—is the first to include other figures. It is accented with indigenous elements, such as the two Khmer-style angels. All the figures are hand-carved from a wood called *daikla*. The Holy Family was carved by Chum Samon and Chay Saron; the youthful kings by Nem Da, Sueh Nduen, and Rottana; and the Khmer angels by Yan Thoun. Other figures are unsigned. The carvers' commitment to creating a special crèche for me adds yet another wonderful dimension to the experience of the collection.

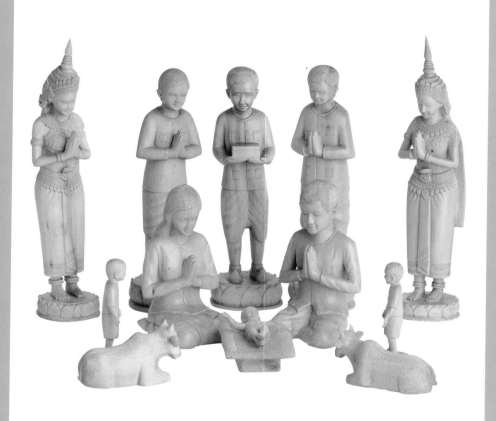

ICELAND
SÓLHEIMAR CRAFTS CENTER

This gaily painted abstract scene, which is also a puzzle, comes from Iceland, where crèches are rare. It was created by learning-disabled people. The small community lives in Sólheimar, not far from Reykjavik, where its members grow vegetables, make jams, and produce crafts, including woodwork. Those with special needs work alongside those without such difficulties. In the wood workshop, established in 1998, a group leader guides the work of community members. The work is divided by the stages of the process: one individual sands, another paints, and so on. The individual tasks may change from day to day, making this colorful crèche truly a group effort.

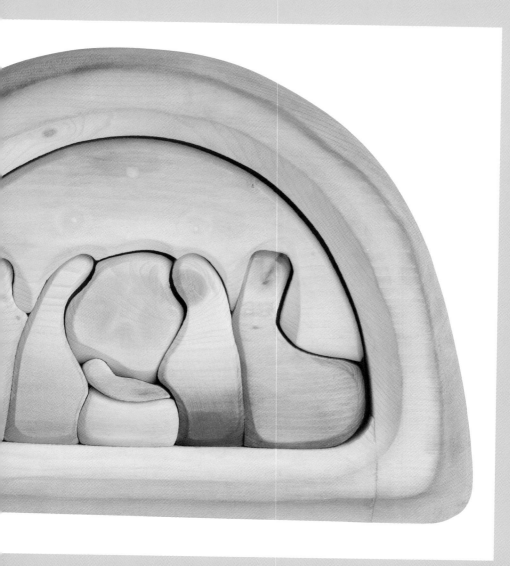

A WORLD OF CRÈCHES

✦

SEEING OURSELVES

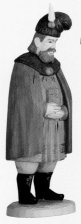

The truth of legends comes from the fact that we recognize in them our own stories and ourselves. This is how the story of Christ's birth has been embellished and elaborated throughout the centuries. The words of the Gospels supply the facts, but art and culture—and faith—the world over provide the details.

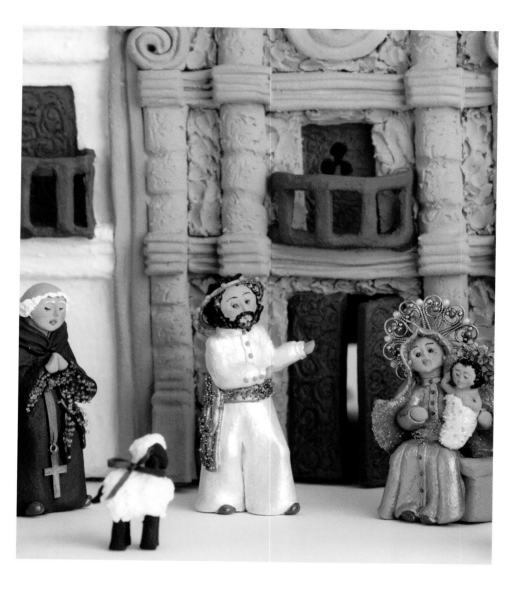

AUSTRALIA
ADRIAN HUNT/JILLI ROBERTS

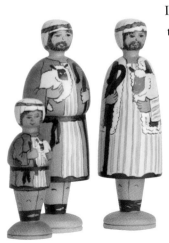

This crèche comes from the wood-turning workshop the Deeping Dolls, which Adrian and Roslyn Hunt established in 1983 in Nicholls Rivulet, Tasmania (it is now owned by others). Adrian was the wood-turner; Roslyn handled the marketing. Inspired by traditional European wooden dolls, Adrian developed his own style.

In the late 1980s, he added crèches to his creations, at first working in three styles: rustic, naïve, and elaborate. In 2001, he introduced an Australian pioneer style, and he occasionally made "Byzantine" crèches. He used only Tasmanian white sassafras, a light-colored softwood once commonly used for clothespins. His figures were painted by professional painters.

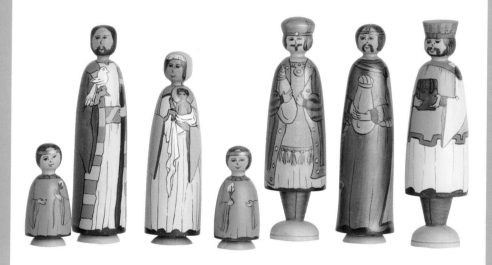

This crèche, turned by Adrian, is painted in the rustic style by Jilli Roberts, the first artist to paint crèche scenes for the workshop. The colors are based on images in stained-glass windows, including those of Wells Cathedral in Somerset, England. Joseph holds a dove, the traditional symbol of peace. Mary holds the Infant, and they are flanked by two blue-clad angels.

NICARAGUA
UNKNOWN ARTIST

This crèche was found for the collection by a USAID colleague. The clay scene was made by a young artist (whose name, unfortunately, is unknown), who won an award for it in an exhibition in Managua. A notable feature of the composition is the disproportionately large Christ Child, who wears a crown. The crown symbolizes Jesus as King; the Infant's exaggerated size also reflects his central importance.

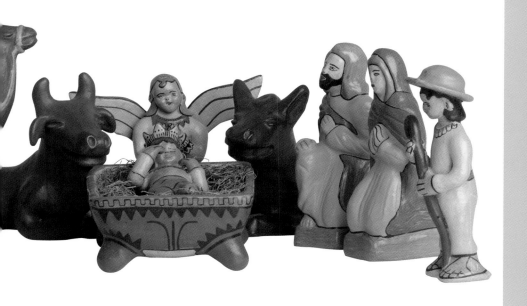

PEПСYLVANIA, USA
JOZEF STACHURA

This crèche was acquired in 1982 at an exhibition in Alexandria, Virginia. Jozef Stachura described it as "unique, made for that show only." Stachura (1923–2001) received most of his education as a sculptor at the Academy of Fine Arts in Warsaw. He joined the Polish resistance during World War II, and was imprisoned by the Nazis. Opposed to Communism, he moved to the United States in 1962. After further study in New York, he became a successful sculptor and teacher. More than 260 of his pieces

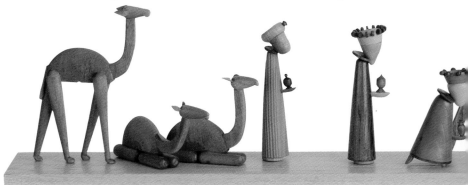

are held in public and private collections throughout the United States and Europe. He worked in many media, especially stone, marble, metal, and wood. Some of his sculptures reflect the sadness and torment of his wartime experiences.

Stachura created many crèches—the first in Poland in 1956—although they account for only a portion of his artistic production. He left them unpainted, but used woods with varying grains and colors, as in the example shown here. Though it bears some resemblance to his earliest crèches, it is much larger; the base measures over 4 feet (1.2 m). The wood's warm, varied tones give the crèche a feeling of depth, despite its linear grouping.

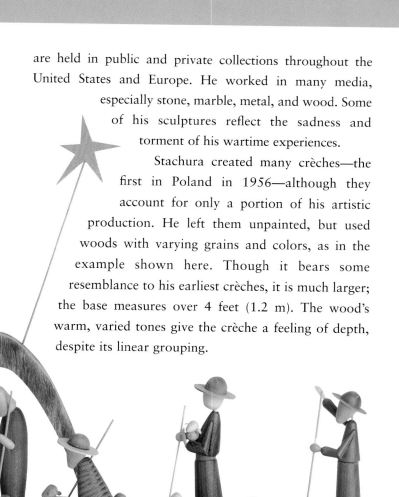

BRAZIL

MIGUEL ÁVILA AND SEBASTIÃO DE ÁVILA

This striking and opulent grouping, commissioned for the collection, reflects the eighteenth-century Portuguese Baroque style. Sebastião de Ávila designed and carved the figures; his brother Miguel worked on details: faces and hands, glass eyes, and polychrome work. Carved and coated with plaster, the figures received an application of gold leaf and decorative incisions. They were then painted and immediately scraped with a stylus-like instrument to reveal the gold underneath.

Both brothers work primarily in wood but also with stone and concrete. Miguel taught himself to work with clay as a boy. He learned much from local *santeros*, and taught Sebastião. Miguel has completed major projects in Rio de Janeiro, Brasília, and São Paulo. Sebastião, whose works are usually smaller-scale than Miguel's, undertakes private commissions and restoration work. Both create mostly religious images.

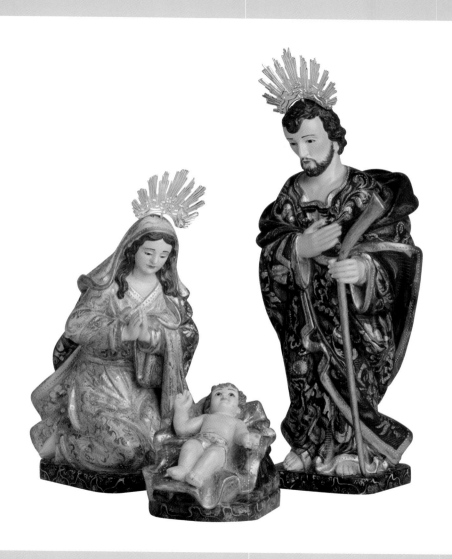

TRINIDAD AND TOBAGO
KEITH SWANSTON

Keith Swanston is a Trinidadian art teacher who carves, sculpts, and paints. His skills derive from a fine-arts education in the United States and perhaps from his heritage; his father worked occasionally with crafts. Swanston considers his own work "a mix of traditional and contemporary." He sculpts in many media—wood, stone, concrete, plaster, and clay—and paints in many media, too. He likes working with the human figure, in a "semi-abstract or abstract form." In 1971, he was named "Best Emerging Artist" by the Trinidad Art Society, and his largest sculpture is on display at the international airport.

Swanston carved this nativity, his first, on commission, and delighted in the challenge. He "let the figures flow naturally out of the shape of the wood" and allowed "one piece to influence the other" as he worked. The nativity, carved from beautiful Trinidad mahogany, is a traditional scene, but reflects Swanston's interest in semi-abstract forms.

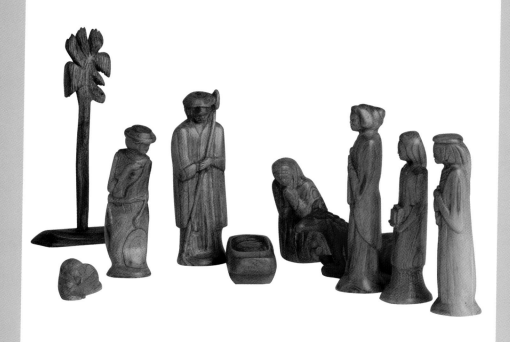

EL SALVADOR

TALLER SAN FRANCISCO DE ASÍS

In the early 1970s, Fernando Llort arrived in La Palma, El Salvador. As a young artist developing his own painting style, he created a center for the study of art and began to teach his style to local artisans, creating a tradition that made the town an arts and crafts center. His workshop's first product was a small nativity painted on a copinol seed. Llort developed a style of simple designs and bold colors, and referred to his craft, which creates an effect similar to enameling, as a "temple" technique.

Even though Llort left in 1979, local artisans have continued to work in this unique style. Brightly hand-painted wooden pieces—including crèches—have now become synonymous with the area. This typically gaily painted scene depicts the Holy Family as *campesinos*, or country people. It was derived from an image in a Puerto Rican cultural publication in 1987, and is produced by the San Francisco de Asis workshop.

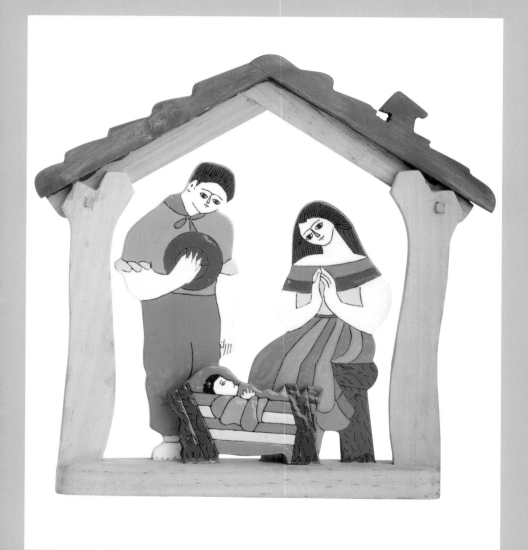

FRANCE
✦
NOËLLE FABRI-CANTI

One of the most impressive crèches in the collection was created by Noëlle Fabri-Canti, and acquired from Monsignor Michael di Tecchia Farina in Washington, D.C. A Corsican-born sculptor, Fabri-Canti is one of France's most celebrated crèche artists, and has been commissioned by Church and Government since the 1940s. Now in her eighties, she has created a legacy of crèches throughout France and especially in Paris, where she has made pieces for such historic churches as the Madeleine. Her scenes are also in Clermont-Ferrand, Tours, and Versailles cathedrals.

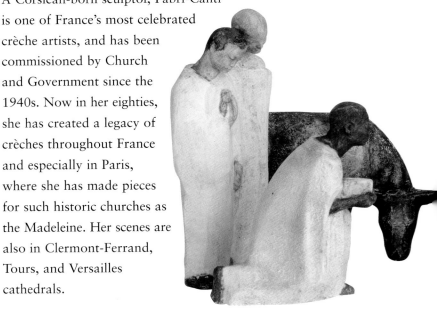

In this clay crèche, typical of Fabri-Canti's style, the figures' simplicity and humble expressions create a sense of peace and stillness. The figure of Mary conveys meekness and gracefulness. Some of the wise men and shepherds seem to have a Far Eastern character. The donkey nuzzles Joseph, adding warmth to the scene, and, most unusually, the Infant is depicted sleeping peacefully on his stomach.

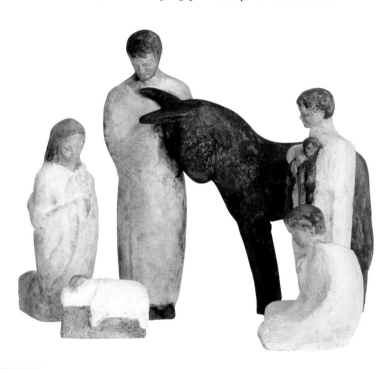

GUATEMALA
UNKNOWN ARTIST

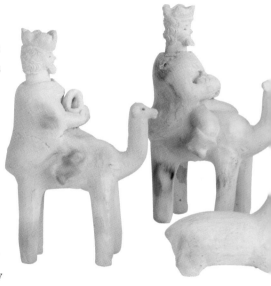

Guatemala is rich in folk-art tradition. This crèche is from Chinautla, one of the country's leading pottery centers. White pottery dating from the time before Christ has been discovered in the region. Mayan artisans in this town continue the tradition of white pottery works, but the clay is now scarcer. Today the pieces are generally made from red clay and then covered with the white.

This finely crafted scene is one of the favorites in the collection. Acquired in the 1970s, it was made by an unknown artisan from Chinautla's "old school." Such

240

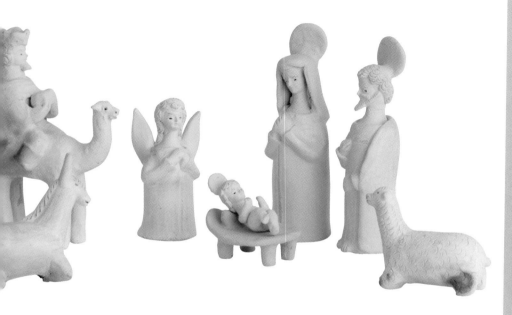

potters carry on traditional techniques, such as molding all pieces by hand, but this one (although handcrafted) is made according to the more recent technique of covering reddish clay with white. A llama-like animal, perhaps a sheep, joins the ox and donkey, and the Infant is in the typical pose of holding out his arms.

HUNGARY
✦
IMRE A. VARGA

Medieval church paintings affected my art very much;
I use their forms and symbolism in an altered way,"
explains self-taught artist Imre A. Varga (born 1953). Varga
considers himself primarily a painter and sculptor. His
characteristic works are what he calls *lada kep* (box
pictures), and this unusual, richly painted crèche is typical,
being set in a box frame. The figures have no facial features,
a device Varga uses to draw attention to their form. The
ladder represents a connection between earth and sky, and
symbolizes how the angel arrived. It reminds us of the
biblical story of Jacob, who saw a ladder that extended
between Heaven and Earth, by which angels descended and
ascended. Another unusual aspect of this composition is
the absence of Joseph, recalling the earliest depictions of the
Nativity. Friends acquired this crèche for me.

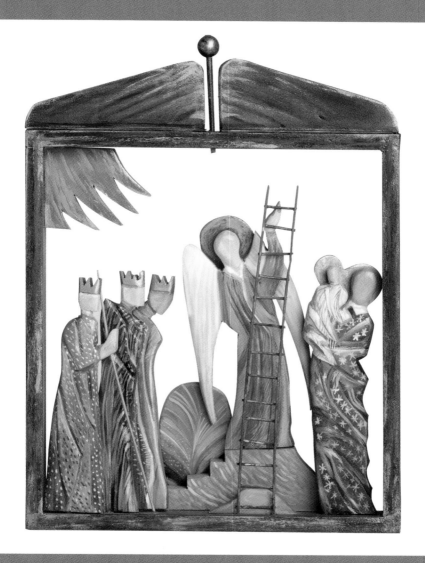

ITALY
*

CAVALiERE GiUSEPPE MAFFEI

Depictions of Christ's birth in local settings are common, but this small nativity is an unusual example. Cavaliere Giuseppe Maffei presents the Nativity in a structure known as a *trullo*. (An artist associate creates the clay figures.) *Trulli* are stone buildings with conical roofs found in the Puglia region of Italy, and Maffei was born in one in 1958. He has devoted his life to creating miniature *trulli*, including nativities, as a way of preserving and spreading knowledge of *trulli* architecture. For his dedicated efforts, especially in traveling to schools throughout Italy to teach children about the tradition, the Italian government

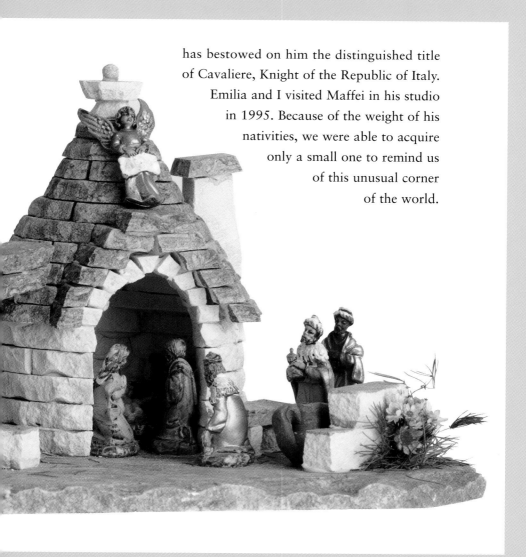

has bestowed on him the distinguished title of Cavaliere, Knight of the Republic of Italy. Emilia and I visited Maffei in his studio in 1995. Because of the weight of his nativities, we were able to acquire only a small one to remind us of this unusual corner of the world.

NEW MEXICO, USA
✦
ELUID LEVI MARTÍNEZ

Eluid Levi Martínez is the grandson of José Dolores López, who revived interest in Spanish Colonial carving (see pages 102–103). Self-taught Martínez (born 1944) observed the work of his uncle, George López, an acclaimed carver. Martínez created his first crèche in 1978, after becoming a water engineer. Dedicated to preserving and documenting both the art of the *santo* and his family's artistic heritage, he encourages Spanish–American artists not to be restrained by the market's desire for reproductions of traditional images, but to apply innovative concepts. The demands of his engineering career have interrupted his art endeavors, but he hopes to resume in the future.

This aspen-wood crèche reflects the family style. Martínez sometimes adds touches of tin or brass, as he has here with the angel's tin wings. The placement of the angel creates a triangular composition, which, Martínez feels, gives an interesting perspective on the Infant.

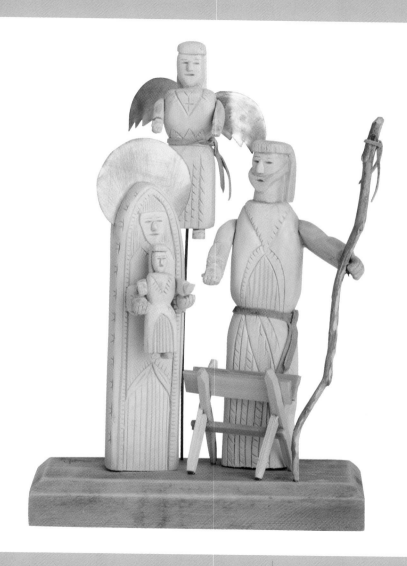

MOLDOVA
STEFAN CIUMASU

This three-dimensional Moldovan nativity scene is a rare example. Moldovans are predominately Orthodox, as is Stefan Ciumasu, and religious imagery traditionally takes the form of icons. Ciumasu (born 1969), who lives in the capital, Chisinau, graduated from a well-known carving school in the Russian village of Bogorodskoye, where the carving tradition dates from the seventeenth century. He earns his living from carving, specializing in wooden animal toys with moving parts, and began creating nativities in 1996.

In this crèche, Ciumasu has created a traditional Moldovan presentation, with Mary, Joseph, and the shepherds in traditional peasants' clothing. Joseph holds a *traista*, a traditional bag, a version of which is still used

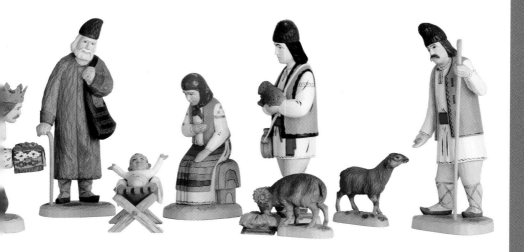

today. One shepherd is feeding a sheep. Two of the kings resemble fourteenth- and fifteenth-century Moldovan knights. The kneeling king is in the image of a fifteenth-century Moldovan monarch, Stefan Cel Mare. The Infant, with arms raised, seems especially joyful.

CHINA
+
WANLONG ZHANG

Wanlong Zhang, a Christian, began carving in 1966 and, twenty years later, gave up making traditional Chinese carvings in favor of Christian-themed ones. Initially he adopted a Western style, but he was encouraged by a Protestant minister in Beijing to carve Christian subjects in the Chinese style. Now he designs Christian art pieces for carving by the artisans in his workshop, which he founded in 1986. One of Zhang's most important projects is a work on the life of Jesus with over one thousand figures in seventy-six biblical scenes. It took more than three years to complete, and was exhibited in Hong Kong in 2004. Zhang's carvings have also been included in several exhibitions in Europe and the United States.

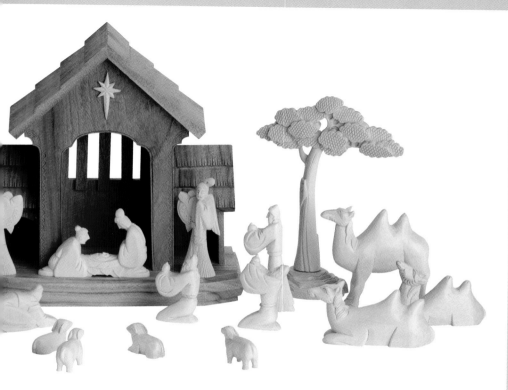

Although small-scale—the delicately carved figures range in size from approximately 2 to 4 inches (5–10 cm) high—this charming nativity strongly shows the indigenous character of Zhang's work, especially in the figures' detailed costumes.

RWANDA
UNKNOWN ARTIST

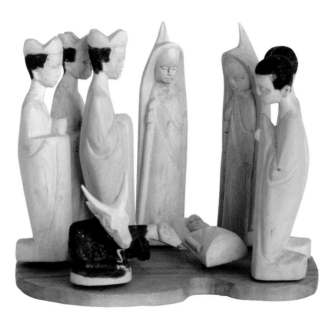

This crèche from Rwanda is a sign that faith and hope are being renewed in this poor country, which suffered so tragically in the 1990s. It is another gift from a USAID colleague.

THE PHILIPPINES
✦
UNKNOWN ARTIST

This traditional wooden scene was probably made by wood-carvers in the town of Paete in the Philippines. Founded in 1580, Paete, like San Antonio de Ibarra in Ecuador, is one of the world's leading wood-carving centers and home to several thousand carvers. Early in the town's history, Franciscan monks helped develop the skills of Paete's artisans, and between them they established a reputation for religious carvings, especially of *santos*. Today carvers continue to make religious images, but they also make furniture and other wooden products.

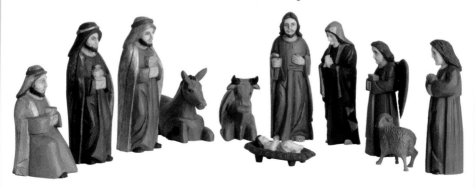

jamaica
+
Lincoln jarrett/
owen grant

The boldly painted animals of this scene evoke Jamaica's vibrant culture, and an intriguing aspect is the ominous presence of Herod, who wears a crown. The figures were carved by Lincoln Jarrett and painted by Owen Grant. Born in 1956 in St. Mary, Jamaica, Jarrett started carving when he was eight years old. He trained as a primary-school teacher, but has worked as a self-taught carver since 1983. Now living in Manchester, in west-central Jamaica, he continues to carve, inspired by Jamaican country life and his religious beliefs. When not carving, he likes to write songs and poems, and he has also tried painting.

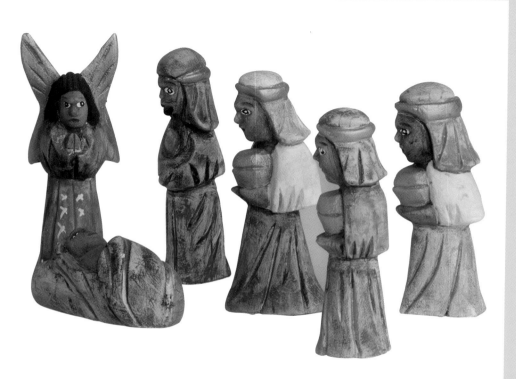

Grant has worked for years with the Gallery of West Indian Art in Montego Bay, where he trained as a painter.

Jarrett carved these figures from Jamaican cedar. His concern for the environment leads him to "encourage the farmers to plant more cedar."

ECUADOR
UNKNOWN ARTIST

This traditional crèche comes from San Antonio de Ibarra. Settled by Spanish craftsmen in the sixteenth and seventeenth centuries, San Antonio remains the most important wood-carving center in South America. The similarity of the style of this crèche to European traditions is clear. The identity of the artist is not known, but the quality of the work suggests that it might have been carved by the late Miguel Herrera, a noted master carver. The light-toned wood is naranjillo.

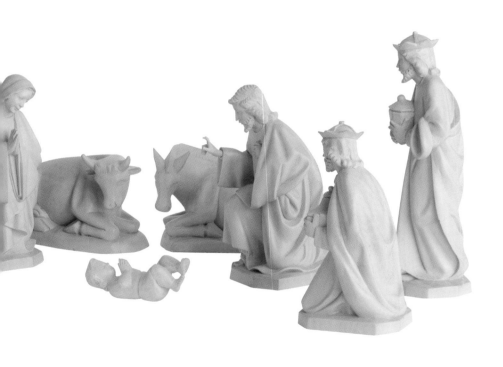

UKRAINE

✦

ELENA URALOVA

This intriguing crèche was commissioned from the self-taught miniaturist Elena Uralova (born 1954) of Lviv, Ukraine. Uralova makes figures no taller than 1 inch (25 mm). A retired civil engineer, she has carved in her free time for nearly twenty years. She began carving crèches in the mid-1990s, when she read the Bible and, as she explains, "came to understand God is great." She claims no religious affiliation, but seeks to use her Christian carvings to promote harmony and peace, aiming her message particularly at children.

Many elements of this crèche are similar to Uralova's usual nativity, but the town scene is inspired by her carving of Christ carrying the cross through Jerusalem. People peer from the finely carved buildings to witness the Nativity. The cloud is adapted from a carving depicting Christ's resurrection. The wood's varied colors give this exquisite crèche warmth. As Uralova says, "I love to create interesting compositions that carry warmth to the people."

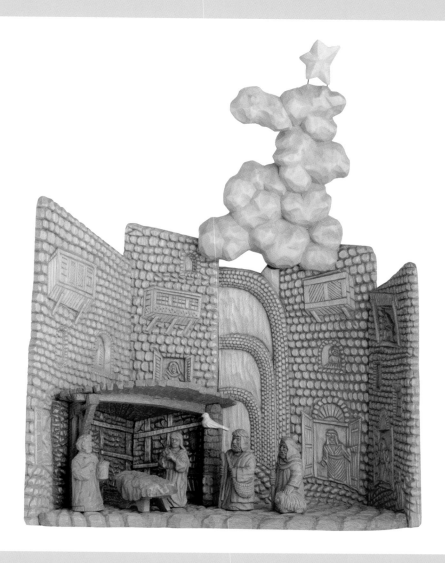

ZIMBABWE
UNKNOWN ARTIST

Little is known about this marvelously carved Holy Family scene, other than its country of origin. The rich wood gives it a luxurious feel. Emilia and I first saw the figures of Mary and Joseph one evening as we walked past a shop in Victoria Falls. Joseph—portrayed as an old man with a balding head—particularly caught our notice. The shop was closed, so we returned early the next morning. Looking again at the two figures, we were surprised to realize that there was no Baby Jesus. The clerk understood very little English and seemed unaware of the concept of a nativity scene, but permitted us to search through the piles of crafts crammed into his shop. After a considerable and intense search, we found the Christ Child in a corner, buried under many other objects. The Holy Family was reunited.

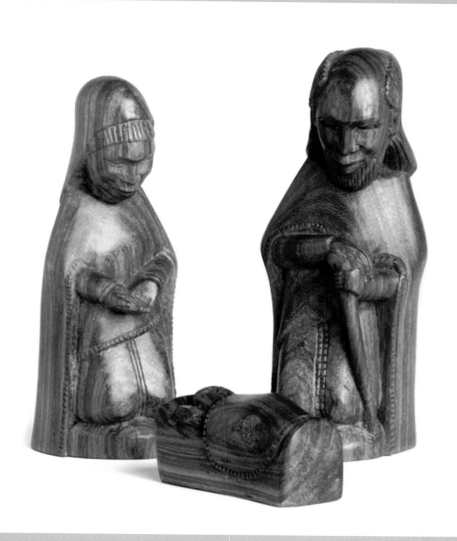

BOTSWANA
✦
PHAKEDI JETA

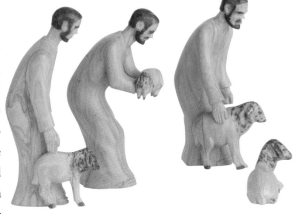

This charming commissioned piece, described as "stunning" by the individual who helped arrange for it to be made, is only the second nativity carved by Phakedi Jeta (born 1963), a bushman who lives in Marulamantsi in northwest Botswana. When he carved this nativity, he was the chair of a group known as the Serowe Woodcarvers, which was trying to establish a successful venture. An adviser had suggested the idea of making a crèche to the carvers, who already made bowls, animals, bushmen figures, and other objects. Jeta has since left the group, but still earns a living from his carving, supporting his five children.

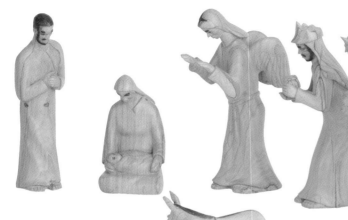
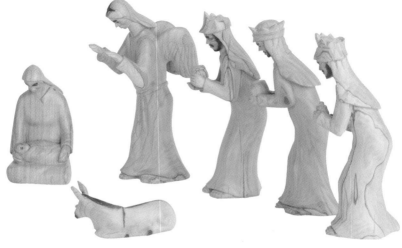

The figures are carved from an attractive wood, modumela, or white syringa. The grain gives flow to the garments, adding to the feeling of movement in the figures of the kings and shepherds. The angel gestures, as if calling attention to the newborn Infant. The painted features of the figures and what seems to be a star on the angel's head are highlighted details in this sensitive scene. "Stunning" indeed seems an appropriate way to describe this crèche.

LATVIA
+
IVARS KALNINS

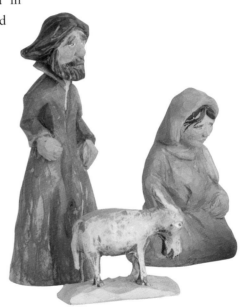

Crèches are not easy to find in Latvia. This one was acquired through the help of a USAID friend and her relatives there. Eventually, her cousin found this scene, carved by Ivars Kalnins. The artist lives in Saulkrasti on the Baltic coast, but occasionally sells his carvings from a street stall in Riga.

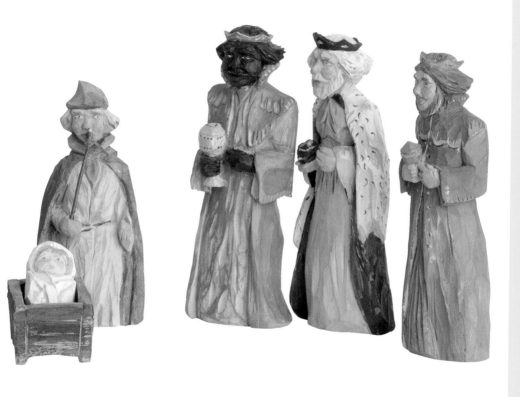

ΠEW MEXICO, USA
JIL GURULÉ

When I commissioned my first crèche from Jil Gurulé (see pages 112–113), I knew she liked to create replicas of historic Southwestern mission churches. I have always been especially attracted to the mission church of San Xavier del Bac, south of Tucson, Arizona. A Jesuit, Father Eusebio Francisco Kino, established the first San Xavier mission in 1700. The present structure, initiated by Franciscan missionaries, was built in 1783–97, probably by the Tohono O'odham people, whom the church still serves.

Gurulé enthusiastically agreed to make another nativity scene, set in the mission. The Holy Family is joined by the wise men and two priests—a Jesuit in black and a Franciscan in blue—and by Native Americans representing the Tohono O'odham, Apache, Hopi, Navajo, and Zuni

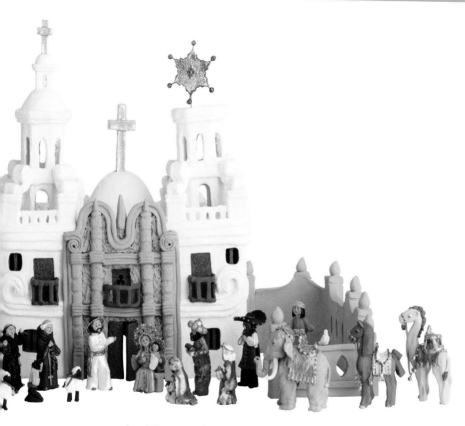

peoples. There is also a Mexican figure. The animals include the donkey on which Mary traveled, as well as a camel, an elephant, and a horse, on which the wise men arrived.

EPILOGUE

Today the universal existence of crèches goes far beyond the expression of faith and devotion that is evidenced in their placement in churches and homes at Christmastime. Certainly, they are made by artists to reflect their faith. They are also made for the market as a means of earning a livelihood by people who, in some places, do not hold the Christian faith. Some artists make crèches primarily to express their culture; others make them as an artistic endeavor.

Out of this varied environment, a rich tapestry of crèche art has emerged. The devotion, creativity, diversity, and skill with which crèches are created have stimulated a renewed interest in the tradition in recent decades. It is an art form that can be appealing as a matter of faith, as an aesthetic creation, or as a familiar cultural expression. Depicting the birth of a child brings all humanity together to share a universal experience. And depicting the birth of the Christ Child brings much of humanity together to share a profound belief in the future.

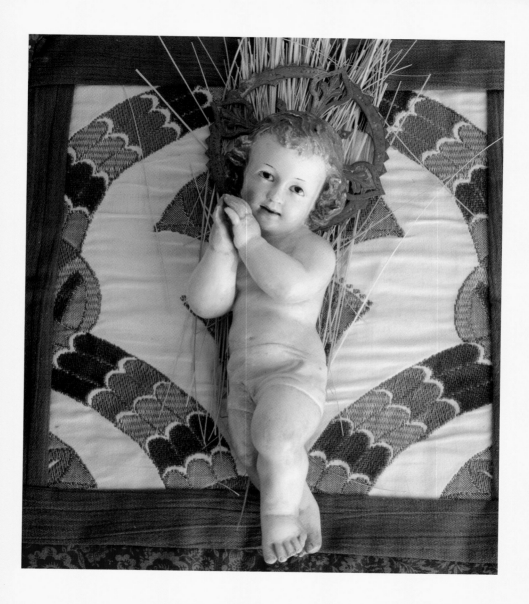

ACKNOWLEDGMENTS

A long-cherished goal is achieved with the publication of this book. The initial purpose of the project, which is based on our Govan family crèche collection, was to celebrate the worldwide crèche tradition. But, with the passing of my beloved wife, Emilia, my desire also became to complete it in her memory. Therefore, first and foremost, I acknowledge her loving partnership in building the collection and initiating the writing. The times we shared each Christmas enjoying the crèches displayed in our home remain among my most cherished memories.

With love, I wish to thank my sons, Michael and Stephen, for their contributions to the collection, and for their support of this project.

I am enormously grateful for the many contributions of Daniel G. Callahan, former Director of Publications and Exhibitions at the Pope John Paul II Cultural Center, which initially supported my effort. Dan's wise guidance and enthusiastic support, as well as his contributions to the structure and content of the book, are deeply appreciated. His steadfast encouragement and determination to assist me in gaining publication of the book were critical to my efforts.

I express much gratitude to Cade Martin for his skillful photography and most cooperative support. I am also most grateful to Gary Ridley of Smarteam Communications Inc., Washington, D.C., whose dedicated technical support in compiling the final text and photography files for